Duchamp, Aesthetics and Capitalism

I0473404

This book is a significant re-thinking of Duchamp's importance in the twenty-first century, taking seriously the readymade as a critical exploration of object-oriented relations under the conditions of consumer capitalism.

The readymade is understood as an act of accelerating art as a discourse, of pushing to the point of excess the philosophical precepts of modern aesthetics on which the notion of art in modernity is based. Julian Haladyn argues for an accelerated Duchamp that speaks to a contemporary condition of art within our era of globalized capitalist production.

Julian Jason Haladyn is an art historian, cultural theorist and professor at OCAD University, Canada.

Routledge Focus on Art History and Visual Studies

Duchamp, Aesthetics and Capitalism

Julian Jason Haladyn

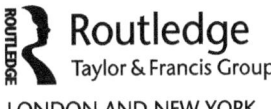

Routledge
Taylor & Francis Group

LONDON AND NEW YORK

Social Sciences and Humanities
Research Council of Canada

Conseil de recherches en
sciences humaines du Canada

Canadä

First published 2020 by Routledge

2 Park Square, Milton Park, Abingdon, Oxon OX14 4RN

605 Third Avenue, New York, NY 10017

Routledge is an imprint of the Taylor & Francis Group, an informa business

First issued in paperback 2022

Library of Congress Cataloging-in-Publication Data
Names: Haladyn, Julian Jason, author.
Title: Duchamp, aesthetics, and capitalism / Julian Jason Haladyn.
Description: New York: Routledge, 2020. | Series: Routledge focus on art and visual studies | Includes bibliographical references and index. |
Summary: "This book is a significant re-thinking of Duchamp's importance in the twenty-first century, taking seriously the readymade as a critical exploration of object-oriented relations under the conditions of consumer capitalism. The readymade is understood as an act of accelerating art as a discourse, of pushing to the point of excess the philosophical precepts of modern aesthetics on which the notion of art in modernity is based. Julian Haladyn argues for an accelerated Duchamp that speaks to a contemporary condition of art within our era of globalized capitalist production"– Provided by publisher.
Identifiers: LCCN 2019025763 (print) | LCCN 2019025764 (ebook) |
ISBN 9780367266769 (hardback) | ISBN 9780367271794 (ebook)
Subjects: LCSH: Duchamp, Marcel, 1887-1968–Criticism and interpretation. | Found objects (Art)–Philosophy. | Capitalism.
Classification: LCC N6853.D8 H335 2020 (print) |
LCC N6853.D8 (ebook) | DDC 745.58/4–dc23
LC record available at https://lccn.loc.gov/2019025763
LC ebook record available at https://lccn.loc.gov/2019025764

ISBN: 978-0-367-26676-9 (hbk)
ISBN: 978-1-03-233818-7 (pbk)
DOI: 10.4324/9780367271794

Typeset in Times New Roman
by Deanta Global Publishing Services, Chennai, India

Contents

vi *Contents*

Figures

Acknowledgments

The author extends his thanks in the first place to Marcel Duchamp, without whose distant collaboration, in the form of his work and ideas, this book could not have been produced. Acknowledgments are due to Michael E. Gardiner, Janice Gurney, Maxwell Hyett, Miriam Jordan, Madeline Lennon, Émilie von Garan and Andy Patton, who generously read and provided commentary at various stages of this manuscript, as well as to Andy Haladyn for his insights into the world of economics and Serkan Özkaya for his inspiring material explorations of Duchamp's artistic ideas. Thanks are due, for their kind support at key moments in this process, to Sara England, Stefan Banz, Michael R. Taylor and Isabella Vitti at Routledge for her backing of this book. This research was generously supported by the Social Sciences and Humanities Research Council of Canada. The author also benefited from the aid of the Research Office at OCAD University, especially Heather Robson, Melissa Golberg and Leila Talei, as well as the Research Assistants who contributed to this project: Émilie von Garan, Emily Lawrence and Maya Wilson-Sanchez. Thanks are also due, for their cooperation, to the Philadelphia Museum of Art, the Israel Museum Jerusalem and the National Gallery of Canada, as well as Serkan Özkaya who went above and beyond. Special acknowledgment is due to Miriam Jordan, whose support and continual encouragement helped guide this project through its at times tumultuous development. This book is dedicated to Miriam.

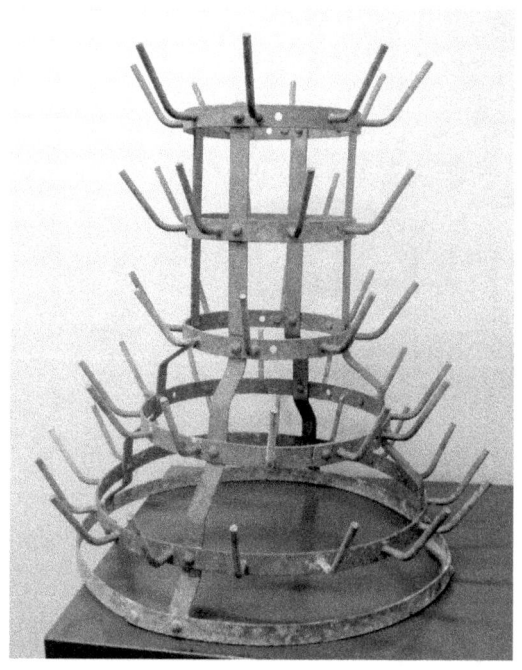

Figure 1 My Bottle Rack, 2018. Galvanized iron 45 × 49 × 49 cm.
Photo by Julian Jason Haladyn.

1 Apropos

No, they're neither art nor non-art. It's not the point. The point is that I wanted to go as far as I could in *doing* art.

– Marcel Duchamp[1]

This is a book not only about ideas of accelerationism but a specifically Duchampian form of accelerationist aesthetics. If, as Steven Shaviro suggests, accelerationism is "the argument that the only way out is through," that overcoming globalized capitalism requires not a withdrawal from it but rather an act of pushing "it to its most extreme point" – which he states is "an aesthetic program first, before it can be a political one" – Duchampian accelerationism describes a specific speeding up of the logic underlying modern aesthetics.[2] It proposes an alternative vision of the notion of accelerating culture, still grounded within a critical approach to capitalist practice, but one that is enacted in and through the concept of the readymade – a mode of artistic production initiated in the early 20th century by Marcel Duchamp.

While regularly viewed as objects of criticism – the readymade challenged the institutional power of the museum to transform an object into 'art' – the acceptability of this mode of art making, which has since become a ubiquitous component in contemporary art practices, has rendered this critique a thing of the past; historical at best, at worst mere *art history*. What does the idea of (almost) putting a pseudonymously signed urinal in an exhibition, an act that took place 100 years ago, say in a world of rampant appropriation and self-conscious, even self-congratulatory simulation? How can the readymade, particularly when associated with the historical personage of the modernist artist *Marcel Duchamp*, have relevance in a day and age when virtually all aspects of our lives are beholden to ready-made products, ready-made experiences, ready-made meanings?

Yet it is this quality of the readymade that is too often overlooked. As a mode of creation, it mimics precisely what we as consumers perpetually do within consumerist society: we choose from the multitude of already existing objects (pre-made *en masse* for the masses) to express our 'self'. The ready-made is not an early 20th-century critique of art – it may have been at one time, but no more. What the readymade has been and continues to be is an act of accelerating art as a discourse, of pushing to the point of excess the philosophical precepts of modern aesthetics on which the notion of art in modernity is based. Duchampian accelerationism is a new way of thinking about objects and art objects within our era of globalized capitalist production.

Notes

1 Marcel Duchamp to Don Bell, "A Conversation with Marcel Duchamp," *Canadian Art* 4.4 (Winter 1987): 57.
2 Steven Shaviro, *No Speed Limit: Three Essays on Accelerationism* (Minneapolis: University of Minnesota Press, 2015), 2; 21.

2   Readymade as object

We begin on the level of the object. To be considered a readymade in the artistic sense, a work must consist primarily or exclusively of an already existing or pre-constructed object, which the work's creator(s) have not produced by their own hands. The artist's act of creation is shifted away from the material production of an object – the physical action of painting a painting or sculpting a sculpture – becoming instead grounded in the moment of an artist's *choice* of this or that object.

For Duchamp, this meant a parade of mass-produced objects from everyday life that he chose to be 'readymades': a wooden stool and a bicycle wheel, a reproduction of an artwork, a snow shovel, a cattle comb, a typewriter cover, a urinal, a bottle rack, a coat rack, a hat rack, a bathing cap and a birdcage, among others. More contemporary enactments of the ready-made aesthetic push this idea of the artist's choice to various extremes – including, as in the case of Sherrie Levine's photographs *After Walker Evans* from the 1980s, the choice of photographing an already existing photograph (of appropriation) or, as in Maurizio Cattelan's formation of a soccer team of North African migrants in Italy *A.C. Furniture Sud* (1991), the choice of recruiting human beings as readymades. Such extensions provide a radical reading of Duchamp's own criteria for selecting his readymades: "The choice was based on a reaction of visual indifference with at the same time a total absence of good or bad taste … in fact a complete anesthesia."[1]

We are a bit ahead of ourselves, but what is important to acknowledge is that the object that will be the readymade exists in the world in some manner, serving a function and all but indifferent to the label 'art', before the artist's act of choosing it. With this choice, the object becomes schizophrenic. While the person creating the readymade may alter the already existing item, perhaps in significant and personal ways, at its base the original 'indifferent' object chosen by the artist remains at the core of the work and working process.

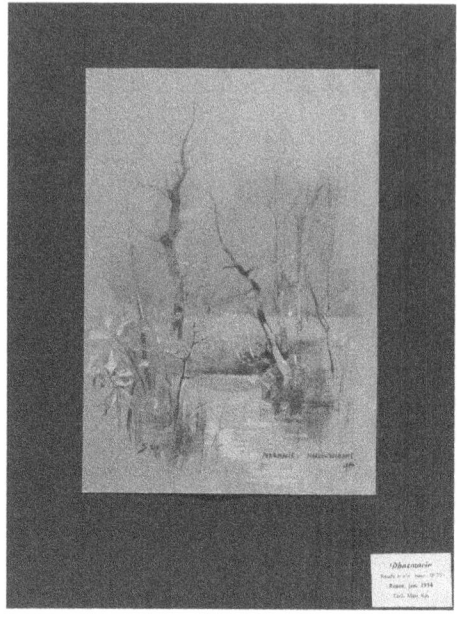

Figure 2 Marcel Duchamp, *Pharmacy* (*Pharmacie*). Reproduction in *From or by Marcel Duchamp or Rrose Sélavy* (*Box in a Valise*) 1935–1941 (contents); 1938 (collotype); deluxe edition, Series A, 1943. Brown leather valise with handle containing sixty-nine miniature replicas and printed reproductions and one original, Virgin (No. 2), 1938, hand-colored collotype. Valise (closed): 40.6 x 37.5 x 10.8 cm (16 x 14 3/4 x 4 1/4 inches) Philadelphia Museum of Art, Louise and Walter Arensberg Collection, 1950-134-934 © Association Marcel Duchamp/ADAGP, Paris/SOCAN, Montreal (2019).

Photo courtesy of the Philadelphia Museum of Art.

If we take as an example *Pharmacy* (1914) (see Figure 2), the object used to create this readymade is a mass-produced chromolithograph of a painted winter landscape at night that Duchamp informs us he purchased – three copies in fact – in an art supply store in Rouen. "It was a commercial print reproduced in thousands of copies, and thus it had the same character as a manufactured object," Duchamp says to Arturo Schwarz.[2] Consisting primarily of bare trees, some stylized flora and a small body of water in the foreground, this traditionally 'beautiful' scene appears to emerge out of the neutral space of the supporting surface, in this case the paper stock of the commercial print, which is also used to denote the snow covering the ground.

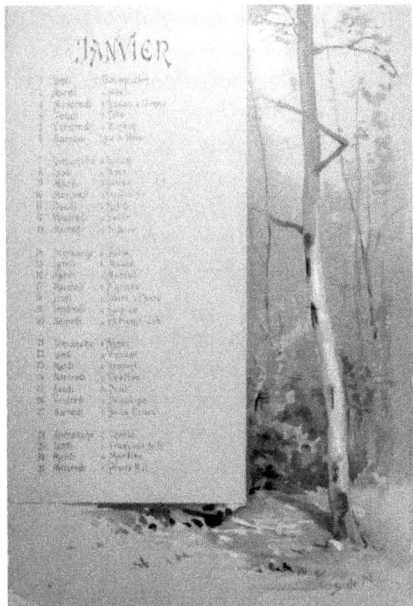

Figure 3 Sophie de Niederhausern, *Calendrier pour 1894*, view of Janvier. Lithograph booklet, published by Damond, Coulin & Cie. 21.5 x 15.3 cm.

Photo by Julian Jason Haladyn.

Of the original artist, there are visible initials in the bottom left within the stylized vegetation that begin with '*S*' and end with '*N*' (see Figure 3); in the middle is most likely '*de*'. While much of the existing literature indicates that this is the work of an unknown artist, some scholars have suggested it is by the Swiss artist Sophie de Niederhausern, which corresponds to the signature.[3] I agree with this suggestion, especially given a comparison between this print and Niederhausern's landscapes reproduced in the 1894 calendar issued by Damond, Coulin & Cie., which show very similar compositions and painting styles, as well as the artist signing her work with '*S de N*'.

Images such as this winter landscape were made available for beginning and amateur artists to copy from, a traditional means of learning artistic techniques and compositions. That Duchamp would choose this object, from an art supply store no less, can be – and has been – interpreted in various ways. What is important for us is to recognize that his choice, since he obviously was not planning on using the image to 'learn' or copy from, plays upon his sense of visual indifference to this type of painting (*qua* reproduction) and approach to art.

To this already existing ('cheap') reproduction of a winter landscape Duchamp added two small dabs of paint on the horizon, slightly off-centred in between the trees: red on the left and yellow and/or green on the right.[4] As Duchamp himself notes on several occasions, the two colours make reference to a traditional image of pharmacies, which in France often displayed bottles of coloured water, red and green characteristically, in their windows.[5] Hence his title, *Pharmacy*, which he writes in the lower right-hand corner of the print followed by his full name (*Marcel Duchamp*), with the year of the work just below. This textual material and the two dots are the only elements separating this object from the multitude of identical images of the winter landscape produced in this batch of reproductions.

While it is typical to focus attention on the differences that distinguish Duchamp's 'art' object from the original object used, I want to first discuss the similarities in these two states. At the base both are produced as part of a series of practically indistinguishable objects that are, for all intents and purposes, interchangeable. The facts that Duchamp would re-reproduce *Pharmacy* in two additional versions, for his *Boîte-en-valise* (1935–1941) and for the 1945 deluxe edition of *View* magazine, and that these re-reproductions have been at times treated in the Duchampian literature as if they were the original 1914 version point to the extent of this interchangeability (on an historical scale) – the hallmark of a ready-made mode of artistic production. The point is that if Duchamp bought a copy of the winter landscape in two separate art supply stores, even in different cities or countries, both versions of the object would provide the same experience, quite literally allowing him to remake his readymade with, similarly, little to no difference from a previous version.

Like the mass-produced objects that constitute the bulk of them, the readymades are for the most part equally (in potential) reproducible. If Duchamp's sisters threw one of his readymades in the trash, *Bottle Rack* (1914) for instance, he could go to a store or send someone else in his place, purchase another bottle drying rack and remake *Bottle Rack* – often by only reinscribing the short textual component he loved to add – with this new version "delivering the same message" as the previous one(s).[6] It is this quality of the readymade, this fundamental "lack of uniqueness" as he described it, that makes this mode of artistic creation so similar to the consumption of objects in consumer society, and also what brings it in line with accelerationist aesthetics.

Notes

1   Marcel Duchamp, "Apropos of 'Readymades'," *The Writings of Marcel Duchamp*, eds. Michel Sanouillet and Elmer Peterson (New York: Da Capo, 1973), 141.
2   Marcel Duchamp, quoted in Arturo Schwarz, *The Complete Works of Marcel Duchamp* (New York: Delano Greenidge Editions, 1997), 597.

3 In the English literature on Duchamp, see the following two references: Jennifer Gough-Cooper and Jacques Caumont, "Ephemerides on and about Marcel Duchamp and Rrose Sélavy, 1887–1968," in *Marcel Duchamp Work and Life*, ed. Pontus Hulten (Cambridge: MIT Press, 1993), np [entry for 4 April 1914]; Stefan Banz, *Marcel Duchamp: Pharmacie* (Cully: Kunsthalle Marcel Duchamp, 2013), 173, 179, 185.

4 In true Duchampian style, there has been some debate about the colour of the dot on the right-hand side. In some versions it appears yellow; this possibility is supported by his statement in "Apropos of 'Readymades'," which lists the colours in *Pharmacy* as red and yellow. In other versions this dot looks green; this possibility is also supported by numerous claims, including statements made by the artist to Jean Neyens and Pierre Cabanne; it is also the 'official' colour listed in Schwarz's *The Complete Works of Marcel Duchamp*. Dalia Judovitz avoids this historical discrepancy by describing the dot as yellow-green, covering both possibilities at once. I have opted instead to heighten this problem – which, we need to consider, was a problem created by the artist himself (through act or word) – by using the Duchampian phrase 'and/or'.

5 Duchamp, "Apropos of 'Readymades'," 141.

6 Duchamp, "Apropos of 'Readymades'," 142.

3 Capitalist accelerations

Let us talk just about objects as they are predominantly conceived and experienced within a culture of late capitalism. I speak here of those encounters with concrete forms that make their presence known to us, that are available to our senses, that frame and materially define the core of our lived sense of reality, of what is really tangible in our world. This is the raw material of everyday life, from the bed we sleep in to the clothes we wear, from the food we eat to the computers and electronic devices through which we define and access the digital world. Often understood as *goods*, these objects in varying ways serve within capitalist systems of valuation as an 'objective' language of things – which in the modern world "are annihilated by their own value."[1]

The material existence of such objects is placed under the erasure of simulation, denied any status except as always-already-replaceable products of a reproducible model – a *simulacra of simulation*, in Jean Baudrillard's terms. As he describes this third-order simulacra: "There is no more counterfeiting of an original ... and no more pure series"; instead, "there are models from which all forms proceed according to modulated differences."[2] Such a conception of the object signals its accelerationism, particularly in the aesthetic state. We may deny that the objects we surround ourselves with accelerate consumerist tendencies, but the overt replaceability that infects them is undeniable and relates solely to the desire to quicken one's experience.

I am reminded of a saying by my grandfather, "it still works," which speaks to a way of seeing objects based on a thing's ability to *work*; that is, to literally continue to do what it was constructed to do or to be put to use in another way. If it could at all be used for something, my grandfather believed it was *useful*. For many of us in this age of mass and technological consumption the question of the value of use – reflecting a Marxist conception of use-value but less concerned with defining it through models of strict consumption – is extremely limited, if not completely subsumed into the issue of progress and advancement. We change computers and phones not because they do not actually work but because we want something new, which is often justified by a desire for something that works 'better' or 'faster'. In the case of computing devices, the issue of it *working* is often irrelevant in the face of the faster, more 'advanced' machines that have greater capacities. Even when such advancements are not needed, even when they are quite literally useless for our personal needs and abilities, this drive for a technological acceleration is core to how we understand ourselves in and through our electronic devices.

In fact, a product that continues to *work* is now a deterrent, especially on the level of economic investments within a neoliberal economy. An iPad that continues to fulfill my needs, that is well-made and does not encourage or require me to purchase the newest model, is a problem in the current business environment of ever-increasing and expanding sales (following the newest myth of 'infinite growth'). In such an environment, the object cannot be understood as having a connection to the value of its true or actual use, or in relation to an original experience that might give it a sense of meaning outside its symbolic and exchangeable status.

Under the current neoliberal mode of consumer capitalism choice is a compulsion tied not to questions of use or even pleasure, except fleeting or short term. Instead, choice within this system is directly connected with the production of never-ending desire on the part of the individual. Within such an economy, the object is irrelevant, a black hole of subjective affects and emotions that are fetishistically fulfilled (momentarily) in the act of consumption. As Alex Williams and Nick Srnicek write in "#Accelerate: Manifesto for an Accelerationist Politics": "Relentless iterations of the same basic product sustain marginal consumer demand at the expense of human acceleration."[3]

For Williams and Srnicek, acceleration is a strategy for positing a constructed future against the imposed limits of capitalism, which has foreclosed a subjective sense of and belief in a futurity. More broadly, theories of accelerationism strategically insist "that the only radical political response to capitalism is not to protest, disrupt, or critique, nor to await its demise at the hands of its own contradictions, but to accelerate its uprooting, alienating, decoding, abstractive tendencies."[4] Many critics see the resurgence of ideas of acceleration, which historically defined the core project of the Italian Futurists, as a result of the publication of three books by French scholars, all published in the 1970s: Gilles Deleuze and Félix Guattari's *Anti-Oedipus: Capitalism and Schizophrenia*, Jean-François Lyotard's *Libidinal Economy* and Baudrillard's *Symbolic Exchange and Death*. (It is significant to note that Guattari, Lyotard and Baudrillard each wrote directly on Duchamp's art and ideas.) Expressly building upon the groundwork of these texts, Benjamin Noys defines the term accelerationism as the tendency "to radicalize capitalism itself," in which the only way to *crash* through the barrier of capitalist production is "by turning capitalism against itself."[5] In place of resistance, accelerationist strategies seek to challenge capitalism by pushing its logic to an absurd extreme.

How does this relate to the object in contemporary culture? While an accelerationist politics only concerns the object in terms of its functioning, how it is instrumentalized in the structures of consumer capitalist culture, an accelerationist aesthetics allows us to consider the speeding up of the object through both its experiential and materialized consequences. "Accelerationism is a speculative movement that seeks to extrapolate the entire globalized neoliberal capitalist order," which for Shaviro means "it is necessarily an aesthetic movement as well as a political one."[6] Signaling the accelerationism of the object is to define its role in accelerating consumerist tendencies and its speculative capacities, tied to its status as a simulation, to aesthetically reflect (double) experience. In fact, the imposed limitations of capitalism are more readily apparent when considering the always-already-replaceable status of the object, which purposively mimics the already-given roles of subjective engagement that are possible within the proscribed limits. To choose an object – to purchase an iPad – is not enough within the current neoliberal economy, we must continue to rechoose, that is repeatedly to repurchase the same or similar objects over and over again. Such is the condition of an object within advanced consumer capitalism: always already replaced by its doppelganger.

How does this relate to art? We like to believe that art objects are completely unique in their material existence, different than the rest of the objects that inhabit our lives. Duchamp was aware of the falseness of this (modernist) conviction. Yet this did not take away from his belief in the vital role of art in modern culture, quite the opposite. On one hand, he clearly appreciated the privileges provided by the label 'art' – even, as with *Fountain* (1917), when he challenged the limitations applied to this category of creation that he thought should be open to anyone. On the other hand, this openness eliminates much of the perceived distinctions between art objects and non-art or everyday objects, undermining the privileged status of 'art' as a category. It is this schizophrenic identity of art under modernity – consistently using its privileged status in relation to life to question why it is not part of everyday life – that the readymade mobilizes on the level of the object and its relationship with the viewer. The readymade confronts not the similarity or difference between art and non-art objects, but rather the ways in which these distinguishing labels affect our understanding and experience *of* a given object.

Notes

1   Roberto Esposito, *Persons and Things*, trans. Zakiya Hanafi (Cambridge: Polity Press, 2016), 81.
2   Jean Baudrillard, *Symbolic Exchange and Death*, trans. Iain Hamilton Grant (London: Sage Publications, 1993), 56.

3 Alex Williams and Nick Srnicek, "#Accelerate: Manifesto for an Accelerationist Politics," in *#ACCELERATE: The Accelerationist Reader*, eds. Robin Mackay and Armen Avanessian (Falmouth: Urbanomic, 2014), 355.

4 Robin Mackay and Armen Avanessian, Introduction, *#ACCELERATE: The Accelerationist Reader* (Falmouth: Urbanomic, 2014), 4.

5 Benjamin Noys, *The Persistence* of *the Negative: A Critique* of *Contemporary Continental Theory* (Edinburgh: Edinburgh University Press. 2010), 5.

6 Shaviro, *No Speed Limit*, 3.

4   Aesthetics and the object

What are the crucial differences separating art objects from their everyday counterparts? One that is repeatedly made mention of, both negatively and positively, is the modernist idea or ideal of art as divorced from the necessities of life: art as purposeful without practical or utilitarian purpose. This "purposiveness without a purpose," as Immanuel Kant described it, is substantiated through the larger discourse of aesthetics the judgments of which are grounded in "the feeling (of inner sense) of the concerted play of the mental powers as something only capable of being felt."[1] If virtually all objects in the modern world are judged based on the value of their purpose or functionality within lived experience, art objects are judged based upon an ability to exceed their material existence and qualities – a judgment significantly situated within a history of similar aesthetic judgments, what we call art history.

The reason for this can be seen in the role of the aesthetic within modernity, which Peter Bürger tells us "is conceived as a sphere that does not fall under the principle of the maximization of profit prevailing in all spheres of life."[2] "I think that aesthetics exists in a special relationship to political economy," Shaviro writes, "precisely because aesthetics is the one thing that cannot be reduced to political economy."[3] Unlike everyday objects, art objects within a modernist tradition are not reduced to the interest of political or economic factors but instead are authorized through the *inner sense* of individuals' interactions with them, the power of which can only be *felt*, not quantified.

With this differentiation is, as a core tenet of an avant-gardist aesthetic, the need to reconcile the differences that separate art from life, art objects from everyday objects. Let us be clear that this drive is idealist, if not fully romantic. It aims not simply to do away with the need to distinguish between the two categories of experience, art and life, but rather to reach a state within culture that would no longer require objects, like the people who engage with them, to be divided into classes. This push and pull between differentiation and reconciliation directly relates to the valuations of consumer culture as developed beginning in the 19th century, with the commodity[4] functioning as the ultimate expression of the logic of political economy that repeatedly extends beyond the object and onto the individual – especially on the level of lived psychologies. If this is the predominant logic applied to the everyday object, as well as the reified individuals who engage with such objects, the art object always finds itself in the process of attempting to both deny and rethink this logic.

At its most basic, the readymade plays with (even mocks) the differentiation between life and art by showing that, with very little 'work' on the part of the artist, an everyday object can become an art object: purpose can be purposeless. Duchamp could purchase a metal bottle-drying rack at the Paris-based department store Bazar de l'Hôtel de Ville, take it home and, instead of using it to dry wine bottles, make "it a 'Ready-made'" sculpture – even remotely, asking his sister Suzanne to inscribe the object and sign it *"[after] Marcel Duchamp."*[5] In theory, he could even ask another person, Man Ray for example (or he could ask me), to buy the object, to re-purchase the same or a similar bottle rack to make another *ready-made sculpture*. With this gesture the everyday bottle-drying rack is divorced from its purpose or function as object – to dry wine bottles on – and reperceived aesthetically as an art object.

This is accomplished through a strategic acceleration of the internal conflict between aesthetics and political economy, which is enacted in an individual's experience of an (in)different object – one not governed by the interests of purposefulness and profitability. Duchampian accelerationism recognizes in the intensification of the logic of political economy, ruled by profit-based judgments, the possibility of aesthetically pushing beyond the perceived limits of aesthetic experience. In terms of the readymade aesthetic, this is accomplished by accepting the chosen object as a lack – or a *delay* or *refrain* – the substance of which is defined not directly but rather through the affects that surround and create it. Something that Niccolò Machiavelli required for his treatment of the political, *effectual truth* – and Duchamp wants us to judge objects based not on given meanings or ideals, artistic or consumerist, but rather on the truth of their effects on us.

Notes

1 Immanuel Kant, *Critique of Judgement*, trans. James Creed Meredith (Oxford: Oxford University Press, 2007), 57, 59.
2 Peter Bürger, *Theory of the Avant-Garde*, trans. Michael Shaw (Minneapolis: University of Minnesota Press, 2004), 42.
3 Shaviro, *No Speed Limit*, 25.

4 "The commodity is, first of all, an external object, a thing which through its qualities satisfies human needs of whatever kind. The nature of these needs, whether they arise, for example, from the stomach, or the imagination, makes no difference. Nor does it matter here how the thing satisfies man's need, whether directly as a means of subsistence, i.e. an object of consumption, or indirectly as a means of production." Karl Marx, *Capital: A Critique of Political Economy*, Vol. 1, trans. Ben Fowkes (London: Penguin Books, 1990), 125.

5 Marcel Duchamp, *Affectionately, Marcel: The Selected Correspondence of Marcel Duchamp*, eds. Francis M. Naumann and Hector Obalk (Amsterdam: Ludion Press, 2000), 44.

5 Comb

Of all his readymades, Duchamp singled out *Comb* (1916) (see Figure 4) as the one he believed was most successful. The reason for this relates directly to his conception of the readymade as, in the artist's words, "complete anesthesia," having neither good nor bad taste.[1]

> During the 48 years since it was chosen as a readymade, this little iron comb has kept the characteristics of a true readymade: no beauty, no ugliness, nothing particularly esthetic about it … it was not even stolen in all these 48 years![2]

Duchamp celebrates this overall lack of interest in the object as an embodiment of his claims about the readymades as neither art nor non-art.

As he was quite aware, even seemingly neutral objects – a wooden stool, a bicycle wheel, a snow shovel, a typewriter cover, a coat or hat rack, a bathing cap – when you look and think about them repeatedly take on an aesthetic, they become beautiful or ugly to you after some time. This clearly occurred with the urinal of *Fountain*. It may have started off as an object chosen because it rarely if ever draws attention to itself, being a thing tied to one of the body's most basic functions that is performed in the privacy of a (men's) washroom. However, after a surprisingly brief amount of time, in fact almost immediately after the scandal around the work's failed inclusion in the Society of Independent Artists exhibition, this urinal began to be discussed and treated aesthetically. The urinal was compared to the traditional forms of a Madonna and a seated Buddha; in his canonical photograph of this object, Alfred Stieglitz stages it in front of a painting that reflects the formal elements of the urinal itself, inscribing it into the discourse of art. All of this makes it impossible to appreciate the object's non-aesthetical qualities.

Almost all the readymades went through similar transformations during Duchamp's lifetime, becoming highly aestheticized, even treated as art objects. While he found the transubstantiating process (turning object into art) humorous, he did not dissuade this development, agreeing to allow these

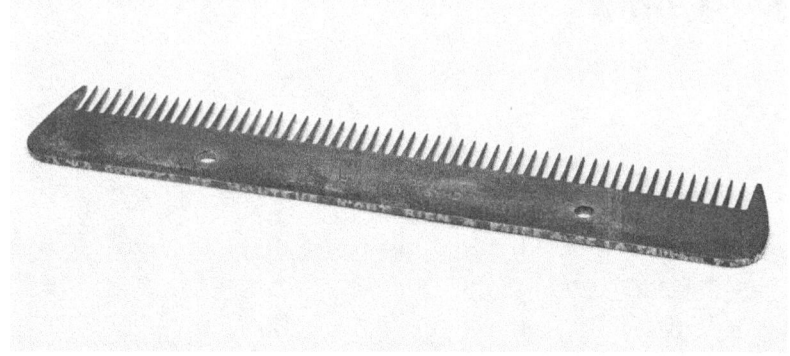

Figure 4 Marcel Duchamp, *Comb* (*Peigne*), 1916. Steel comb and paint. 16.5 × 3.2 × 0.2 cm (6 ½ × 1 ¼ × 1/16 inches). Philadelphia Museum of Art, Louise and Walter Arensberg Collection, 1950-134-72 © Association Marcel Duchamp/ADAGP, Paris/SOCAN, Montreal (2019).

Photo courtesy of the Philadelphia Museum of Art.

anaesthetic objects to be included in numerous art exhibitions, allowing Arturo Schwarz to create limited edition versions of the main readymades, permitting these absent objects – a majority of the 'original' readymades having been lost or destroyed – to become part of collections. All of this served to consecrate the readymade as an art object (art practice) within the history of art. To experience the readymades in the latter half of the 20th century up to the present is to encounter a decidedly aesthetic object with little to no trace of Duchamp's desired indifference.

Comb is the one apparent exception to this new understanding of the readymade. Because of the lack of historical interest in this particular object – which was not even stolen – it had for Duchamp managed to retain an element of anesthesia he was seeking in this way of doing art. As an object, it has none of the complexity of a bottle-drying rack or a mass-produced chromolithograph of a painted winter landscape, none of the promiscuity of a bicycle wheel attached to a stool. The comb is relatively small, materially simple and unassuming, its form eliciting an explicit lack of visual interest (a boredom). This may in part explain why scholarship on this particular readymade object, the specific comb chosen by the artist to be *Comb*, has been less than critical – many historians and theorists continue to identify it as a dog comb, which it is not. This mistake is understandable since Duchamp himself refers to this object as "an ordinary metal dog comb."[3] Yet the material features of this particular comb, its overall design, does not conform to the types used for dogs at that time or after.

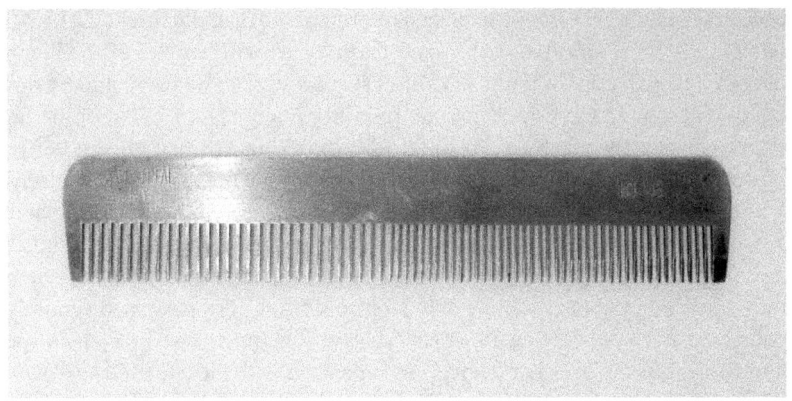

Figure 5 Furrier Comb (A. Westpfal New York City), 1910s. Brass. 16.4 × 2.9 × 0.1 cm (6 ½ inch comb).

Photo by Julian Jason Haladyn.

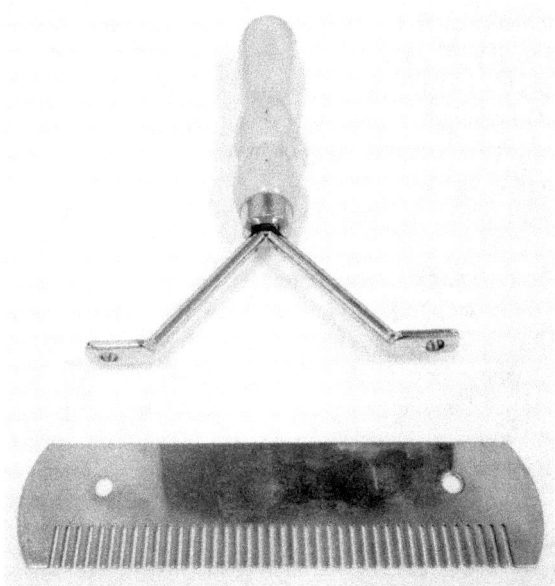

Figure 6 Cattle Comb, 2018. Steel and wood. Whole: 16.2 × 3.3 × 14.6 cm comb [detached]: 3.3 × 14.6 × 0.2 cm.

Photo by Julian Jason Haladyn.

Most telling are the two holes located symmetrically on the flat of the object, which, except for the teeth and imprint of the manufacturer – CHAS-F BINGLER/166 – 6th Ave. N.Y. – are the main visual features of the comb chosen by Duchamp. In terms of overall shape and size, we can compare this comb with a solid brass furrier comb (used for removing knots out of the fur of dogs and cats) made by A. Westpfal, also from New York City in the 1910s; however, the flat of this comb is solid, with an imprint but no holes. Similarly, a Spratts Brass Dog Comb from the 1920s (see Figure 5), made in England, has a number of key differences in terms of form, including again no holes in its surface. In fact, when one does see holes in the flat of any type of comb they most often appear on one side (for holding) or are patterned (entirely decorative). The exception is when they are functional, used to attach the comb to another element or device – as is the case with the one used as *Comb*, which is actually the comb part of a cattle comb that attached with screws or bolts to a handle through the two holes (see Figure 6).

Without the handle, which is needed when combing larger animals such as cattle or horses, it is easy to see how the object can be mistaken (even mistakenly used) as a dog comb. However, it is clear both from the overall material design of the object and the distinctive presence of the holes that it is a type of cattle comb, one that is still generally in use to this day. (I acquired my own cattle comb from an online retailer, the actual comb part bearing a striking resemblance to the one used by Duchamp.)

A few interested spectators have made note of this discrepancy: Kirk Varnedoe and Thomas Girst notably.[4] The error nonetheless persists, even in recent critical and historical publications on Duchamp's work. Such a lack of precision limits the extent to which *Comb* can be examined as an object, not apart from the ideas of the work but also not strictly subsumed within such conceptualities either.

Much attention has been given to the playful text written along the spine of the comb, which reads: 3 OU 4 GOUTTES DE HAUTEUR N'ONT RIEN A FAIRE AVEC LA SAUVAGERIE. This is part of the readymade process for Duchamp. He explains: "One important characteristic was the short sentence which I occasionally inscribed on the 'readymade'. That sentence instead of describing the object like a title was meant to carry the mind of the spectator towards other regions more verbal."[5] Such a moment of text is meant to complement (like complementary colors) the object that is its surface, the two forming a complex balance of the material and imaginative qualities of individual experience. Too much of the scholarship on *Comb* favors these purely conceptual interpretations of the work, with a hint of the psychoanalytic, such as Thierry de Duve's pushing this *peigne* – as "qu'il paignne!" or "let him paint!" – into the figuration of the allegorical.[6] Such interpretative efforts are of course important, but of equal importance is the taking serious of the already existing object Duchamp chose to be this readymade.

Encounters with a particular object, even when they are singular instances of repeatable mass-produced objects, are of great significance to Duchamp. Why else would he insist when asking a friend to create a replacement for the broken *Paris Air* (1919) that "the bulb must be the same size that I gave you because that's the size of the original (broken)"?[7] Why else would he be concerned with the fidelity of the 1964 Schwartz edition of remade ready-mades, insisting that they maintain the details of the specific objects he chose for each? Why else would he write the exact day and time he chose the comb to be a readymade – Feb. 17 1916 11 A.M. – on the actual object? Far from a means to achieving a purely conceptual work, the object is a vital part of the readymade process because it is the matter through which the dialogue of art takes place.

What we experience with *Comb* is a partial object, which, known or not by the artist, is encountered in a disassembled (split) state. We cannot simply pretend that it is a whole and complete object, as has been the case histori-cally. Instead, we should consider the role of this object in our conception and understanding of the work, which leads us away from the problem of original versus copy and instead asks us to look at the moment of art as experience. Following the fact that it is a cattle comb, presented without its handle and previous functionality – doubly so as a readymade – we need to reformulate the limits of this object's potentiality, present and future. This opens up excess material and conceptual possibilities for experiencing this comb's continuing aesthetic refusals.

Notes

1 Duchamp, "Apropos of 'Readymades'," 141.
2 Marcel Duchamp, quoted in *Marcel Duchamp*, eds. Anne d'Harnoncourt and Kynaston McShine (New York and Philadelphia: Museum of Modern Art and Philadelphia Museum of Art, 1973), 279.
3 Marcel Duchamp, "Apropos of Myself," lecture, The Baltimore Museum of Art, February 10, 1963; quoted in *Marcel Duchamp*, eds. d'Harnoncourt and McShine, 279.
4 Kirk Varnedoe and Adam Gopnik, *High and Low: Modern Art, Popular Culture* (New York: Museum of Modern Art and Harry N. Abrams, 1991), 274; Thomas Girst, "Von Readymades und 'Asstricks'," *Tout-Fait: The Marcel Duchamp Studies Online Journal* (2003): http://www.toutfait.com/issues/volume2/issue_5/articles/girst/girst1.html. To these I will add an online source, the blog *appeau vert* [jour-nal] which posted an interesting analysis, "Qu'il peigne à peine," accessed 23 June 2018: http://ap.over-blog.org.over-blog.org/article-19217384.html.
5 Duchamp, "Apropos of 'Readymades'," 141.
6 Thierry de Duve, *Kant After Duchamp* (Cambridge: MIT Press, 1997), 168, 172.
7 Duchamp, *Affectionately, Marcel*, 273–374.

6   Speeding up language

When Duchamp inscribes a short sentence or other form of textual material on a readymade, he provides us the means to carry our minds away from a strictly retinal encounter with the object (just looking) towards an experience more verbal, as he words it, moving us into the realm of language (thinking). This is not an act of literature, with its emphasis on narrative, but one of poetry – Guillaume Apollinaire made a similar observation when the artist was a young man.

On the most basic level, the additions serve to signal a moment of distinction separating the object chosen from others in the same series, with this text in several cases being the only key difference. Without the addition of the playful inscription – (in translation) 3 OR 4 DROPS OF HEIGHT HAVE NOTHING TO DO WITH SAVAGERY – written on the spine of *Comb*, or the initial and date on either end, this comb would appear identical to other metal combs from similar models of cattle combs. The same is true for *Bottle Rack*, which, even though the artist forgot the sentence he composed to write on the first bottle-drying rack he chose, the object continued to be re-inscribed (differentiated even within its own difference). Understanding signature as a form of text, we can also see that without the pseudonymous name and date – R.MUTT 1917 – on *Fountain*, the urinal cannot be substantially differentiated from other similar urinals.

While it may be obvious, we should nonetheless note that these texts do not change the constitution of the object in-itself. The urinal that is *Fountain* remains a urinal and can be put back to use – as contemporary artist Tania Bruguera showed us in 2011.[1] Just as the bottle-drying rack of *Bottle Rack* can still be used to dry bottles, text or no text. It is our perception, our subjective experience of the object that is altered through the addition of textual elements. In fact, there is an intentional falseness to this act of differentiation, which signals a fundamental lack of difference in that, by repeating the inscriptions on a newer model of object, the moment of distinction is transferred (transferable). Duchamp's addition of text onto the bottle-drying rack of *Bottle Rack* does not fundamentally differentiate it from other similar the bottle-drying racks, but instead demonstrates that any bottle drying rack can, potentially, be put to the task of being *Bottle Rack*. We can locate this logic within the appropriated term 'readymade'. In America at the time Duchamp began to call his works by this name, readymade commonly referred to mass-produced clothes that one purchased off-the-rack from a store, as opposed to items of clothing that were tailormade for a specific individual. In his words readymade "means 'completely finished', like off-the-peg garments."[2] The rise of consumer capitalism brought with it a shift in how people related to objects, away from individualized or customized relationships towards generalized or standardized (parameterized) forms that one chooses from, which are sold to us as complete without us. When buying a shirt from a store I am faced with a series of completely finished shirts in particular colours, styles and patterns in pre-existing sizes; while I may want the blue to be a little darker or for the shirt to be slightly larger or smaller, I can only ever choose from among the already-made shirts available. Regardless of this lack of personal preference and input, we are trained by consumer culture to see our act of choosing from among already-existing choices as a moment of defining our individuality, of making self.

Like a person shopping for a shirt, Duchamp creates *Fountain* by selecting from the urinals available to him and choosing one – or having someone make the actual choice for him – that, regardless of personal preference (taste), was obtainable and best suited his needs. And like all other commodity objects, when repeated, the urinal was subject to change depending on the specific models available – the urinal Sidney Janis chose in 1950 is materially different from the one Duchamp first used, but functions as *Fountain* nonetheless. Following this logic, Duchamp quite literally expresses his creative self by claiming a relationship with a pre-existing object that he played no role in actually making but which he authorizes through the fact that he chose it. (These are the exact words he used to defend the fictitious Richard Mutt who submitted the urinal as an 'art' object for exhibition.) If "accelerationism experiments with the possibility of speeding up and intensifying capitalist relations and ways of living, exacerbating its dissolutions and its velocities, until something breaks," we can see in Duchamp's readymade mode of artistic production an acceleration of capitalist understandings of the relation of subjects and objects.[3] With the adding of textual elements maximum exacerbation within the readymade process is achieved, marking the moment when the chosen object is actively refused its 'completeness', which includes also refusing it its difference.

Beyond simply isolating a single object chosen from among many, the repeatability of this act of inscription on these repeatable objects makes it clear that his specific use of language does not add but rather takes away from the object. Carol P. James describes this conflict:

> When the readymade is named as such and text becomes part of it, a new relationship of writing and the visual is created. The text takes the readymade out of its ordinary writing framework as something immediately recognizable by its place or function, and the object forces the reader to temporarily abandon reading as a discursive activity that relates to a non-present. The object distorts, or anamorphizes, the frame of reading and the text displaces the (up until now) recognizable object into a non-place where art and everyday life mix and one can no longer be told from the other.[4]

This is less a merging (of art and life) and more a moment of contradiction, of conflict between the visual and the textual that is presented to the spectator From Marcel, as he loved to sign his work. If the readymade is a rendezvous, Duchamp wants to make sure it is always an incomplete one.

The short sentences and other written elements inscribed on the object of the readymade were not meant as didactic or descriptive (literary), but rather as abstract and poetic fragments that complicate the relation of the spectator to the artwork. By adding the nonsensical phrase on the spine of *Comb*, Duchamp denies us a simple one-to-one relationship with this (once) cattle comb – and I am personally surprised at the lengths to which art historians will go to regain this relationship. On one hand, we look at the readymade as an object, talk about its misuse as an art object and negotiate or even attempt to erase this difference. On the other hand, we read the inscription on this object, automatically and almost involuntarily trying to make a connection between the playful phrase and the object that is its ground.

On one hand, *Apolinère Enameled* (1916–1917) [Figure 7] is a commercial advertisement for the industrial paint Sapolin Enamel that is corrected or rectified by Duchamp, or more precisely for us from Duchamp. The actual image is a charming scene of a young girl painting the frame of a bed in her room, showing us the ease of using this ready-made product – that even a child can paint with it. To and from this completely finished object, Duchamp adds and subtracts elements, exacerbating the abstracting modernist (consumerist) sensibilities played out through the poetic relationship of a young girl – "who wields a paint brush as she would her comb (her hair, sketched in by Duchamp, is reflected in a mirror)" – and her (presently useless) bed. James suggests that this "is a sort of allegory of the readymade where artists who paint ('peignent') give up their brushes to choose everyday objects like the comb ('peigne')."[5] Completeness is rendered partial through these rectifications.

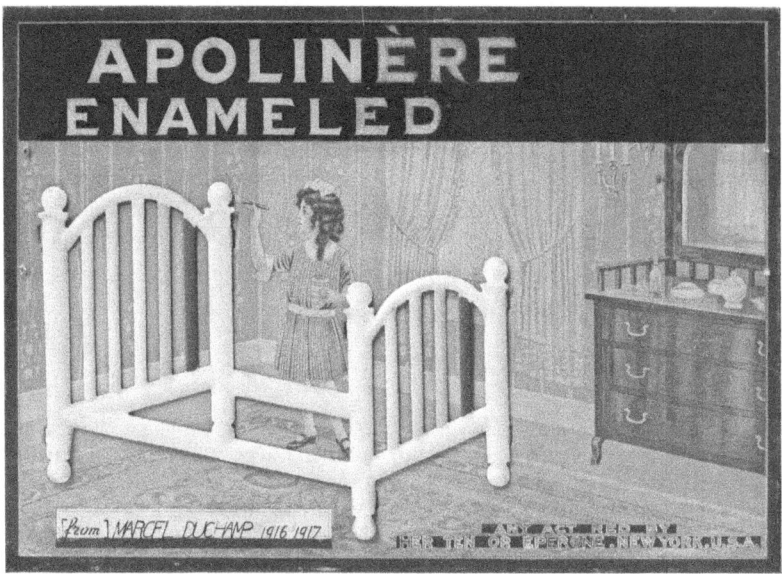

Figure 7 Marcel Duchamp, *Apolinère Enameled*, 1916–1917. Gouache and graphite on painted tin, mounted on cardboard. 24.4 × 34 cm (9 5/8 × 13 3/8 inches). Philadelphia Museum of Art, Louise and Walter Arensberg Collection, 1950-134-73 © Association Marcel Duchamp/ADAGP, Paris/SOCAN, Montreal (2019).

Photo courtesy of the Philadelphia Museum of Art.

On the other hand, *Apolinère Enameled* is an amalgam of wordplays that overwrite the pictured scene. Duchamp alters the name of the company, presented in a black band across the top of the image, deleting (painting over) the letter 'S' from SAPOLIN and adding 'ÈRE' to "intentionally" misspell the name of the eminent poet Guillaume Apollinaire, and adding 'ED' to spell ENAMELED.[6] This rather direct acknowledgment of Apollinaire (as Apolinère with a glossy coating), a person who had an undeniable impact on Duchamp's conception and treatment of language – not the least for introducing him to the practice of the eccentric writer Raymond Roussel[7] – positions the work as a type of poetic tribute. To this blatant re-writing (as historiography) Duchamp also adds a small playful phrase – ANY ART RED BY HER TEN OR EPERGNE, NEW YORK, U.S.A. – bottom right, rearranging the letters of name and city of the company; on the left is his signature, which tells us the work is 'from' Marcel Duchamp.

Language signals the confluence of contradictory meanings that intensify the necessity for what he refers to in one of his notes – the most profound expression of his poetic conception of language – as the "counderstanding of opposites."[8] Part of this 'counderstanding' is an acceptance of the transferability of differentiated differences, which defines the critical moment when we both have access to the (already existing) object and are positioned to rectify it for our selves. The fragments of text found on readymades purport meaning yet refuse to simply give it to the viewer turned reader, instead presenting language as a challenge to the individual spectator's relationship with the object. Duchamp is helping us on our way to creating subjective meanings in our encounter with these everyday objects (turned art objects), but only we can actualize meaning for ourselves by thinking through the object.

Notes

1 As part of her development of *Arte Útil*, or *useful art*, Bruguera chose a urinal similar to one used by Duchamp, inscribed it with 'R. Mutt', and installed it as a functioning plumbing fixture in a men's room at the Queens Museum of Art. "I have always said that we have to put Duchamp's urinal back in the restroom. Now that urinal is in the restroom of the Queens Museum, you can see it and pee on it." Tania Bruguera, "Introduction on Useful Art," taniabruguera.com (23 April 2011): www.taniabruguera.com/cms/528-0-Introduction+on+Useful+Art.htm.

2 Duchamp to Philippe Collin, "Marcel Duchamp Talking about Readymades" [interview 21 June 1967], in *Marcel Duchamp*, ed. Museum Jean Tinguely (Ostfildern: Hatje Cantz, 2002), 37.

3 Gean Moreno, "Notes on the Inorganic, Part II: Terminal Velocity," *e-flux journal* 32 (February 2012): www.e-flux.com.

4 Carol P. James, "Duchamp's Early Readymades: The Erasure of Boundaries Between Literature and the Other Arts," *Perspectives on Contemporary Literature* 13 (1987): 27.

5 James, "Duchamp's Early Readymades," 26.

6 Duchamp, "Apropos of Myself"; quoted in *Marcel Duchamp*, eds. d'Harnoncourt and McShine, 280.

7 In a 1949 letter to Jean Suquet, Duchamp stresses "how indebted I am to Raymond Roussel who, in 1912, delivered me from a whole 'physicoplastic' past which I had been trying to get out of. A production at the Antoine theater of 'Impressions d'Afrique' which I went to see with Apollinaire and Picabia in October or November 1912 … was a revelation for the three of us, for it really was about a new man at a new time." Duchamp, *Affectionately, Marcel*, 283.

8 Marcel Duchamp, *Marcel Duchamp, Notes*, arranged and translated by Paul Matisse (Paris: Centre Georges Pompidou, 1980), np. See note 185.

7 Challenges to origineity

With the readymade, we witness in the minimal distinction of the chosen object from its serial counterparts an accelerationist aesthetic that, first, accepts the object in its commodified form – Duchamp does not resist or fight the fact that it is mass-produced for sale within consumerist culture – second, works with the internal logic of the object to produce an artwork that reflects the principles of its reproducible nature.

We can compare Duchamp's engagement with already existing objects to those of his contemporaries, especially the Surrealist interest in the found object and the creation of Surrealist objects. While the two approaches are often conflated, treated as generally the same type of act, there are core differences that separate these practices. Chief among these is the fact that the Surrealist object still participates within the economy of the original, whereas the readymade does not. As Margaret Iversen notes, "While the readymade is essentially indifferent, multiple, and mass-produced, the found object is essentially singular or irreplaceable, and both lost and found."[1] If, for example, Meret Oppenheim's *Object (Breakfast in Fur)* (1936) was destroyed, the work would be lost and could only continue existing in material form as copy – with the museum tag listing the work as a replica of the original. This object, like all Surrealist objects, is created by an 'artist' just like a painting or sculpture, and therefore its existence is fundamentally (or logically) singular.

The readymade does not conform to this logic, being neither solely created by the artist – the object pre-exists the artist's use of it – nor limited to a singular existence. If Duchamp's *Fountain* was lost or destroyed, which was not an uncommon occurrence during his lifetime, the 'artwork' titled *Fountain* did not change in any significant manner. When the urinal of the *Fountain* pictured in Alfred Stieglitz's famous photograph from 1917 was discarded or lost, this did not prevent other urinals from becoming *Fountain*. For example, when Sidney Janis decided to include the work in his 1950 exhibition *Challenge and Defy*, he asked the artist to sign a urinal he had found – Janis purportedly picked this object up in Paris at a flea market. Another example is the version of *Fountain* Ulf Linde created for the 1963 exhibition in Stockholm he organized, the focus of which was the readymade; in Adina Kamien-Kazhdan's account, Linde had noticed a urinal similar to the original "in the men's room of the Italian restaurant Fratis Tre Remmare," which he had "removed, disinfected, and signed 'R. MUTT 1917' using self-adhesive block letter and numbers."[2] And each of these urinals has had a life as *Fountain* to the present day: the former in the Philadelphia Museum of Art and the latter in Stockholm's Moderna Museet (now with Duchamp's actual signature, which he, after removing the lettering, inscribed when he saw the version in person).

To state the obvious, the singular artwork Fountain exists as a plurality of objects that each contribute to a type of multitudinal existence. All the readymades share this quality of one concept or idea being many (in potential) objects, with the important caveat that this process is without a true origin – or, as in the case of a temporal paradox, the beginning is first realized in the viewer in response to experiencing the (art)object. The readymade aesthetic is the basic principle of this foundational lack of origineity (the quality of being original), so that Walter Benjamin's famous articulation of reproduction is reversed through the gesture that sees a plurality of reproduced objects take on a series of individualized unique existences. Duchamp actively celebrated this status and, as we see in his correspondence, enlisted others to help him create additional readymade eventualities; let us look at two moments.

In preparation for the 1959 exhibition *Art and the Found Object*, Duchamp asks Man Ray to send him the bottle-drying rack, or bottle dryer as he refers to it, which will be used as the current version of *Bottle Rack*. In his letter, Duchamp writes: "If you've lost it, maybe buy another one at the Bazar de l'Hôtel de Ville."[3] Not having the bottle dryer in his possession, Man Ray followed Duchamp's instructions and went to the bazar. There he bought four bottle-drying racks of varying sizes, which allowed Duchamp to choose the one that most conformed to the work *Bottle Rack*.

May 1949, Duchamp writes two letters to his friend Henri-Pierre Roché in which he discusses the reconstitution of *Paris Air* (1919) (see Figure 8). In the first he writes:

> May I ask you the following favour. Walter Arensberg has broken his ampoule, 'Paris Air'. I've promised him I'd replace it. Could you go into the pharmacy on the corner of rue Blomet and the rue de Vaugirard (if it's still there, that's where I bought the first ampoule) and buy an ampoule like this one: 125c.c. and the same measurements as the drawing. Ask the pharmacist to empty it of its contents and seal the glass with a blow torch. The wrap it up and send it to me here.

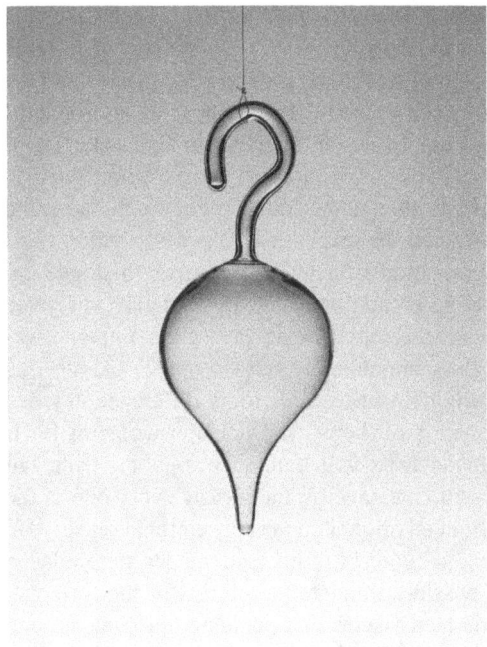

Figure 8 Marcel Duchamp, *50 cc of Paris Air*, 1949. Glass ampoule. 15.2 cm (6 inches). Philadelphia Museum of Art, Louise and Walter Arensberg Collection, 1950-134-78a © Association Marcel Duchamp/ADAGP, Paris/SOCAN, Montreal (2019).

Photo courtesy of the Philadelphia Museum of Art.

In the follow-up letter, he explains:

> Yes, the bulb must be the same size that I gave you because that's the size of the original (broken). The ones in the box-valises are miniatures, like all reproductions (in general). Have one made for yourself at the same time.[4]

This final statement is particularly interesting, giving a clear sense that for Duchamp the actual objects that constitute the readymades lacked the preciousness or singular valuations of a typically (original) work of art.

None of the urinals of *Fountain* or the bottle drying racks of *Bottle Rack* or the glass ampoules of *Paris Air* in museums today are by definition original, especially in the artistic (or Duchamp's own) understanding of the term. Neither, in any iteration one might encounter, are the bicycle wheel and stool of *Bicycle Wheel* (1913), the shovel of *In Advance of a Broken Arm* (1915), the Underwood typewriter cover of *Traveler's Folding Item* (1916), the coat rack of *Trap* (1917) or the hat rack of *Hat Rack* (1917); the same would be true of the rubber bathing cap of *Sculpture for Traveling* (1918) and the geometry textbook of *Unhappy Readymade* (1919) if they were in museums. Nor are the readymades always identified on the museum tags as copies or replicas, a common practice for stand-ins of 'original' works of art. We may note that the version of *Paris Air* located in the collection of the Philadelphia Museum of Art, which is considered the main version, is described as 'broken and later restored', a categorization reflected in Schwarz's catalogue raisonné and most of the scholarship around the work; this is humorous given that 'restored' in this case means the initial ('original') glass ampoule was physically replaced by a new glass ampoule.

The fact that they are not originals makes little to no difference in terms of the experience and interpretation of the work. Duchamp writes in 1961: "Another aspect of the 'readymade' is its lack of uniqueness ... the replica of a 'readymade' delivering the same message; in fact nearly every one of the 'readymades' existing today is not an original in the conventional sense."[5] He puts this claim to the test when, in 1964, 14 of his readymades are produced in editions that as closely as possible simulate the objects of the 'original' readymades; it is these remade readymades that populate museums around the world. The aesthetic of the readymade functions not through the logic of the original but instead through that of simulation or simulacra.

How to characterize this logic: Baudrillard will locate the question (law) of value in the moment of repetition, when, unlike the first order of simulation that sees the original counterfeited or the second order that enacts a pure series, in the logic of this third order simulation

> there are models from which all forms proceed according to modulated differences. Only affiliation to the model has any meaning, since nothing proceeds in accordance with its end any more, but issues instead from the model, the 'signifier of reference', functioning as a foregone, and the only credible, conclusion.[6]

"Simulation is no longer that of a territory, a referential being or a substance. It is the generation by models of a real without origin or reality: a hyperreal."[7] Through the logic of simulation, experiences of value and meaning are tied not to origineity but rather to hyperreal – Duchamp might say infrathin (or *inframince*) – interpretations based within the model.

With the readymade we witness an infrathin distinction between the everyday object and the art object, a moment of separation that is infinitesimal. Defined strictly through example, Duchamp in a note will characterize this notion in relation to consumer production: "The difference / (dimensional) between / 2 mass produced objects / [from the / same mold] / is an infra thin / when maximum (?) / precision is / obtained."[8] Hence, the hyperreality of an object generated through a model and without origin or reality – such as a mass-produced urinal or bottle drying rack or cattle comb – one that is singled out from the series and always already replaced by another from the series, its difference from these serial counterparts is infrathin. For Duchamp, this distinction can only take place in and through the spectator's encounter with this infrathin occurrence.

With the readymade mode of artistic production the work is not the object in-itself but rather the model or conceptual template for the creation of the artwork. This process, as Duchamp liked to say, is necessarily fulfilled on the level of the spectator's engagement and interpretations, which "brings the work in contact with the external world."[9] This is why the work can be repeated without being experienced as a mere copy or replica, why we are able to get the same message from different iterations or versions of a Duchampian readymade – such as when I viewed *Bicycle Wheel* at the Philadelphia Museum of Art and then, later that same day, at the Museum of Modern Art in New York City. For Duchamp, it is the model that defines the moment of 'art'.

Notes

1 Margaret Iversen, "Readymade, Found Object, Photograph," *Art Journal* 63.2 (Summer 2004): 50.
2 Adina Kamien-Kazhdan, *Remaking the Readymade: Duchamp, Man Ray, and the Conundrum of the Replica* (London: Routledge, 2018), 96–97.
3 Duchamp, *Affectionately, Marcel*, 358–359.
4 Duchamp, *Affectionately, Marcel*, 273–374.
5 Duchamp, "Apropos of 'Readymades'," 142.
6 Baudrillard, *Symbolic Exchange and Death*, 56.
7 Jean Baudrillard, *Simulations*, trans. Paul Foss, Paul Patton and Philip Beitchman (New York: Semiotext(e), 1983), 2.
8 Duchamp, *Marcel Duchamp, Notes*, np. See note 18.
9 Marcel Duchamp, "The Creative Act," *The Writings of Marcel Duchamp*, eds. Michel Sanouillet and Elmer Peterson (New York: Da Capo, 1973), 140.

8   Consequences of a Duchampian accelerationism [1]

Acutely and strategically accelerating the overall parameters of the aesthetic encounter in modernity, the Duchampian readymade forces us to recognize the latent possibilities that surround experiences of objects (consumer, everyday and art). These are not qualities of the object in-itself, nor are they to be found *in* the object's material form as the colloquial wording implies. The qualities that the readymade highlights are in fact not actualized anywhere that can be related in a direct or blatant way to the object in question, but must instead be understood as manifest in and through the individual's experience when engaging with the object. This aesthetic envisioning of the subject has two important consequences that define the parameters of a Duchampian accelerationism.

In the first of these, we must accept the overtly subjective nature of experience under modernity. This is defined most powerfully in Kant's theorization of a modern aesthetics that is a language of inner sense, capable of speaking to a world the determining ground of which is purely subjective; experiencing an object therefore begins not in the world but rather in the mind that interprets (and necessarily corrects) the information of the senses; it must begin with the subject's creative acts of representing, the point of reference being constituted in the subject, not the object. Duchamp's own concepts of the creative act follow a similar logic, in which the defining of the qualities and capacities of an artwork – expressive as well as historical – begins not with the artist who makes the art object but rather with the (world) spectator whose job it is, willingly or unwillingly, to interpret the inner qualifications of the (art)object as it exists apart from the artist.

It thus falls on us to aesthetically judge the readymades, to make them more than the mere objects chosen by Duchamp – to make them 'art'. Suffice it to say, without the innumerable spectators who, over the past 100 years, viewed *Fountain* and judged (even through the acceptance of the common sense or mass judgments of culture) that it is a work of art, as opposed to just a urinal in a museum, it would not be 'art' today. The same process in fact occurs with all artworks, except that the rarefied nature of the material product – traditional art mediums such as paintings, drawing and sculptures – blinds us to the necessity of our role in justifying the label 'art' being applied to a particular object. This is why Duchamp's use of non-unique products helps us see this act of aesthetic transubstantiation. Such an understanding allows art as a discourse to exceed itself, because it requires onlookers to not simply accept a *given* object and experience but rather to creatively make such encounters subjectively real within their own time and place in the world.

We must add a caution at this point. Addressing excess in terms of the artists themselves, on the level of production, can be misleading if we fail to situate the larger experiencing of the object within late capitalist, especially neoliberal, modes of thinking. As Shaviro notes, "Neoliberalism has no problem with excess. Far from being subversive, transgression today is entirely normative."[1] The increasing commercial and economic success of art post-1980s, particularly its attempts to produce 'radical' and 'subversive' products, demonstrates how easy it is for an artist's challenge to be used as a marketing ploy. On the level of reception, however, the idea of excess is more poignant because, as Duchamp realized, it must confront the *actual* (as aesthetic gap) – again, willingly or unwillingly. We can recall the words of Maurizio Lazzarato, "The readymade continues to surprise precisely because it continues to challenge our present actuality."[2] To state this directly: the creative act exists as a potentiality that the artist manifests into an object of possibility, which is actualized by the spectator only after is it subjectively interpreted into the world of individual experience.

The readymade crystalizes this understanding by presenting an object devoid of inherent 'art' production and instead manifesting excess potential and possibility, so much so that it requires the label of 'art' to begin the distillation process that the spectator must undertake. Duchamp's proud claim of *indifference* here becomes the boredom of possibilities in modern culture, where choice is positioned as the ultimate (consumerist) creative act – one that he, rather than accepting or rejecting, transforms by locating it within the realm of the aesthetic. We are indoctrinated to believe our choice of one shirt or couch or car over another is an expression of individuality, with a sleight of hand making sure we do not question this simplistic remainder. Capitalist society from the 19th century to the present is about teaching people to think and act through ready-made possibilities, and art's attempted resistance to such limitations, through avant-gardist and neo-avant-gardist aesthetic strategies, have proven for the most part insufficient in the face of everyday needs and desires.

Duchamp's readymade aesthetic is different from avant-gardist tendencies. It functions through virtually the same process of choice as that exercised within everyday life under consumer capitalism, in which one of innumerable possible objects is raised to the status of 'special' by the act of individual selection. The fact that *Fountain is that particular urinal*, as opposed to all the other urinals that represent the products of that model, makes one believe it is special, it is 'art' – and the other urinals with modulated differences are not. Duchamp intentionally undermined this through his blatant foregrounding of the work's repeatability. *Fountain* has been and continues to be many different urinals, each enacting their own particular manifestation of this creative act.

The reproduced landscape of *Pharmacy* is special because it was the one picked out, chosen by the great artist *Marcel Duchamp*. Within the logic of the original, this is no different from the fact that my couch is special to me because it is the one I selected, as opposed to all the others that I did not: *me*, of course, being the determining factor distinguishing the one from the multitude. The significance of the specific reproduction Duchamp chose to be *Pharmacy* is only extant after its selection (after he *rectified* the object). This understanding is applied to the experience of the object through a recognition of the artist's act of choosing it, which necessarily happens in opposition to the many acts of choosing, by unknown individuals, the same reproduction of the winter landscape from the same art supply store in Rouen – or, as is the nature of reproductions, from any other location in which it may be found for purchase. The adding of the two dots and textual material by Duchamp, far from making this object distinct and 'original', signals the mere attribution of the sign of individuality through traces of (mental) experience with the object, an attribution that can easily be repeated with a similar product from this same model.

To repeat: the replacement of the physical object of the reproduced landscape within another following this model does not actually affect the act of signification, rather it challenges the idea of 'art', or more generally creative meaning, as understood through the necessarily *original* product of the artist. Duchamp's readymade mode of art making speeds up the creative act by putting it into dialogue with processes we all engage in when choosing reproducible consumer objects from a store (physical or online), except with the added element of self-conscious aestheticization that requires a critical mode of choice-making.

Notes

1 Shaviro, *No Speed Limit*, 31.
2 Maurizio Lazzarato, *Marcel Duchamp and the Refusal to Work* (Los Angeles: Semiotext(e), 2014), 20.

9   The choice economy

The first consequence of Duchampian accelerationism is grounded in a base understanding of the object within everyday consumer capitalist society, which in a contemporary context no longer addresses itself to questions of production (proper) or objectification. Instead, the object speaks to meta-actualizations demanded through the conditions of subjective choice that are the categorical imperative or ultimate commandment of *Homo economicus*, an obligatory drive defined through the (moral) necessity to make choices. This is the choice economy.

In his discussion of money and power flows, Lazzarato argues that *purchasing power*, "which represents the entirety of means of payment (wages and revenue) used in the buying of goods already produced, already present," is strictly subordinate to the prescriptive *power of financing*, which is "a set of possibilities for choices and decisions with regard to the future, which anticipate what the production, power relations, and forms of subjection will be."[1] It is not the ready-made object or the labor of its production that drives the economic core of late-capitalism, but rather the subjectively driven emblem of personal choice. While consumer products appear to us as a panoply of individualized needs and desires, providing what can seem like unlimited varieties of possibilities to choose from – faced with shelf upon self of innumerable boxes of cereal or cellphone covers – the limits of these choices are determined before our encounter; I cannot, for example, purchase a cereal or cellphone cover that does not exist. The power of choice is allocated to those who define its limits, who construct the existing economy that necessarily contains and controls all choices within its bounds. If once tied to ideals of free will, choice in an age of capitalist democracy functions through shared idiosyncratic decisions among innumerable already-existing mass-products and pre-determined actions.

"The recent trend in sociology and economics is," Remo Bodei writes in *The Life of Things, The Love of Things*,

> to downplay the negative effects of consumerism, to no longer consider, for example, the consumer as a passive, heterodirected individual, a victim of advertising, but rather as an active subject, who, with his own choices, assigns value to the world in which he lives.[2]

The power of the choice economy rests on the compulsive need for individuals not simply to choose, but, more invasively, capitalism's demand that such decisions actively imbue the chosen objects with immanent and inner personal meanings, which (as it turns out) must be repeatedly replenished. Choice begets choice – without which, subjective meaning is experienced as a missed experience. A couch or iPad or reproduction of an artwork is not considered meaningful apart from individual experiences of – or more properly projections of such experiences onto – these things, which are mere iterations of their model. And such meanings are in fact conceived as (ideally) reproducible, replaceable *ad infinitum*. I can always buy another couch or iPad; even when it is not exactly the same product, it serves the same function and becomes significant and meaningful in similar ways as the last model through my acts of experiencing it, of interpreting it into my world.

No different from the variations among the manifestations of Duchamp's readymades. If we look closely at all of the existing versions of *Fountain* that are associated with the name of *Marcel Duchamp*, that is, official versions on display in major museums and collections, we see what are a number of totally different objects. While all are flat-back urinals, the form of the 1917 version and 1964 remade version based on this 'original' are sharper with flatter surfaces, whereas the 1950 (Sidney Janis) and 1963 (Ulf Linde) versions both are more fluid with rounded surfaces. The latter *Fountains* are visually quite simple with an overall smooth and curving surface, whereas the former *Fountains* include two incised lines around the back – the base when it sits on a pedestal – and a raised edge running across the top of the lip that defines the opening (the space into which one urinates) of this lavatory feature. Even the drainage holes differ, collectively forming a triangle in one case and a circle in another. Yet all these versions, no matter the differences in their form, still serve the model of the artwork *Fountain*.

Rather than an engagement with (critical or otherwise) *purchasing power* as derived from the treatment of already present products, a meaningful encounter with *Fountain* is directly related to its active engagement with and exaggeration of *financing power* as anticipating productions through the quagmires of capitalist choice. What I face when I stand in front of *Fountain*, any version of *Fountain*, is not the object that is the mass-produced and commercially sold

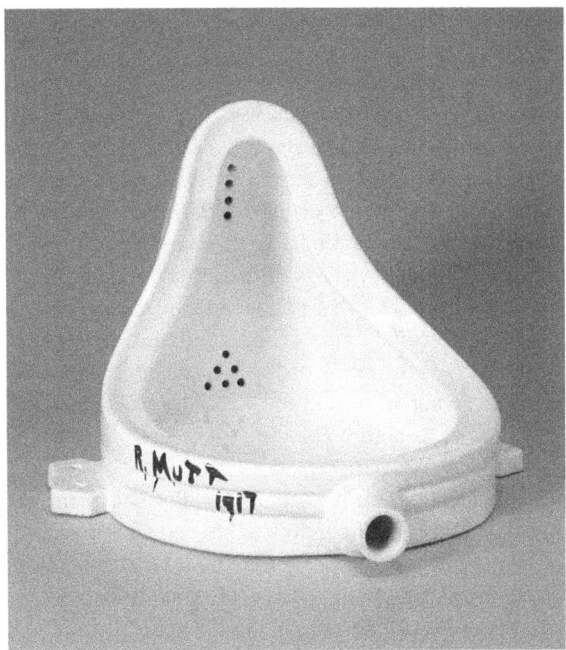

Figure 9 Marcel Duchamp, *Fountain*, 1964 [5th version]. Glazed ceramic white ware with black oil paint. 36 x 48 x 61 cm. National Gallery of Canada, Ottawa © Association Marcel Duchamp / ADAGP, Paris / SOCAN, Montreal (2019).

Photo courtesy of the National Gallery of Canada.

urinal on display – nor, in the case of the remade readymades of the 1960s, is it the reproduced mass-produced object (see Figure 9). Instead, what I face is a model of the choice economy that produces the possibilities of this readymade mode of production. Not the meaning or value of the art object but rather the production of the possibility of artistic meanings and valuations.

I am thinking here of Louis Althusser's conception of *interpellation*. Not in the way David Joselit understands and uses the idea – looking at strategies of the Duchampian readymade as 'hailings' of existing identities temporarily qualified through the *object-as-self* and *self-as-object*, but as a reading that explicitly looks beyond issues of reification.[3] Regardless, it still remains entrenched within the larger subject-object dualities, which locate the readymade within questions and possibilities of production on the level of the deterritorialized object. My claim is that the readymade, not the already present object but the set of possibilities defined through its idea – for example, the idea *Fountain*, which can and does exist in relation to multiple displayed urinals – acts in such a way that it recruits or transforms onlookers into creative subjects that serve to define its existence as 'art'.

The unique quality of the readymade as non-unique or anti-originary, especially its use of blatantly reproduced and reproducible objects, demands the creative subject be a self-conscious subject. It is also important to the process that these objects exist simultaneously within two parallel discourses: modern art and modern everyday culture, which includes consumer culture. (These discourses share a complex history within modernity, both investing in modes of evaluating the relationship of subject and object.) Self-consciousness enables a critical awareness of the artist's acts of choice in – not producing – choosing an object that is not 'art' to be an object of art. Additionally, it means that spectators must at the same time be aware of their own role in choosing to accept the readymade object as 'art', especially knowing that the same object is not within other discourses or contexts. In truth, each of us each time we stand before *Fountain* make it art by viewing it, accepting it as such.

The readymade aesthetic places a premium on choice. For Duchamp, the power of choice making is the ability of the individual to actualize possibilities through judgments, by making a choice – by making future choices. Yet within an environment of consumer capitalist excess, in which subjectivity is located within the seemingly unlimited varieties of possible objects (material and so-called immaterial), choice has become an existential crisis. Such a crisis applies to the treatment of all manner of objects, including the art object. As contemporary artist Geoffrey Farmer unequivocally states: "The terror for me is to have to make one choice."

Farmer makes this confession in relation to his collage-installation *Leaves of Grass* (2012), a work constructed out of thousands of photo-based images taken from issues of *Life* magazine. Installed as a series of shallow sculptural layers of images mounted on small wooden poles, arranged in a narrow base along on a long table, this project presents a chronology of human history between the dates of 1935 and 1985, as defined by one popular culture publication. It appears as an overwhelming jumble of visual information. Farmer continues:

> it was to have a multitude, an encyclopedic number of things with which to play around, to juxtapose, to arrange, to order or to disorder. That impulse has been to present what could be a cosmology. Also, I believe it is a way that I deal with some anxieties I have about the scale of things, in a cosmological sense. It allows me not to have anxiety about making choices. How can you be anxious about making one out of a multitude of choices? If I spread them out it seems easier to make a choice or even to forget that I am making choices at all. But more importantly it is a way

for me to express the absolute awe that I have for the complexity and diversity of our experience.[4]

Here the image as object is treated as an impossibility of choosing, because making just one choice necessarily constrains and excludes – fearful words in a culture of capitalist democracy. Farmer's acts of choice are in fact celebratory acts of *non-choice*, an aesthetics of accumulation that attempts to avoid the responsibility of choosing by replacing it with the production of repeated and repeatable "choices" that end only through exhaustion.

This exhaustion, caused by the (existential) crisis of having to choose *one out of a multitude of choices*, of having to actively exclude possible experiences, is the core symptom of the choice economy. Byung-Chul Han will characterize this as the violence of positivity, which "does not deprive, it saturates; it doesn't execute, it exhausts."[5] This problematic is based within the economy of choice that defines much of the experience within the lives of people living under late capitalism, which actively attempts to replace responsibility – *should* I make this choice – with possibility – *can* I make this choice? Lyotard will describe this in terms of Duchamp's practice:

> There is causality because you have to give a why of the choice made between several possible realizations. It is ironic because you have to invent, choose the why that you've given. So there is a choice to be made among the whys. The irony consists in the reversal: you affirm the why of the choice (of realizations); you suggest furthermore a choice of this why. To justify the choice is to transform consistency into necessity or permission into obligation; it's to pass from the "it's possible" to the "it's necessary."[6]

This for Lyotard is Duchamp's *hinge logic*.

Here a less dramatic enactment of interpellation occurs everyday at the moment we encounter and, more importantly, interpret ideas into the objects we surround ourselves with in an orgy of consumption. These are not police officers hailing, *hey, you there*; these are shiny electronic devices, useless curiosities, bright ads on our smartphones calling to us with unknown and novel identities that we are given to choose from – personalized advertisements for personalized consumption. These are objects that hail us with promises of a singular, unitary experience of self. Meaning is in this way the ultimate manifestation of authority in modernity because we are made to believe meaning is found, purchased, a quality of the objects we are convinced to purchase over and over again. We are made to believe that without ready-made consumable objects life, our life, is meaningless.

The readymade aesthetic suggests an alternative approach. Duchamp's readymades ask us: What if we could understand that meaning is created, not found? What if we could see in our acts of choice the power of valuation, enabling (empowering) us to repeat or revise the entire universe? What if we could recognize that objects are gaps in experience, models of possibilities for subjective choices and decisions as opposed to moments of objective interpellation? What if we can experience art not as the meaning of objects on display but rather the meanings made possible through the ideas that surround our encounters with the object?

Notes

1 Maurizio Lazzarato, *The Making of the Indebted Man: An Essay on the Neoliberal Condition*, trans. Joshua David Jordan (Los Angeles: Semiotext(e), 2012), 83–84.
2 Remo Bodei, *The Life of Things, The Love of Things*, trans. Murtha Baca (New York: Fordham University Press, 2015), 67.
3 David Joselit, *Infinite Regress: Marcel Duchamp 1910–1941* (Cambridge: The MIT Press, 1998), 196.
4 Geoffrey Farmer to Robert Enright (with Meeka Walsh), "The Multitudinous See," *Border Crossings* 36.1 [issue 141] (March 2017): 28.
5 Byung-Chul Han, *The Burnout Society*, trans. Erik Butler (Stanford: Stanford Briefs, 2015), 7.
6 Jean-François Lyotard, *Duchamp's TRANS/formers*, trans. Ian McLeod (Venice: Lapis Press, 1990), 119.

10 Readymade as black hole

Gilles Deleuze and Félix Guattari discuss what they call the black hole (function) in several parts of *A Thousand Plateaus*, connecting it to the vital concept of strata – "acts of capture" similar to "occlusions striving to seize whatever comes within their reach" – and pairing it with the white wall. They describe this system: "Significance is never without a white wall upon which it inscribes its signs and redundancies. Subjectification is never without a black hole in which it lodges its consciousness, passion, and redundancies."[1] This black hole is machinic, it is psychological; it demands recognition not for what it is, which is a lack or gap, an extent spatial and/or temporal absence, but rather in and through the effects of its presence on the consciousness of its surroundings. The black hole is futurity, but a futurity – very much like the readymade – devoid of the need for subjectified exhaustion.

Duchamp's practice historically took part in many of the same cultural pressures as the Italian Futurists, artists who define the core of an early 20th-century push to accelerate culture – *speed* for them is a form of beauty. Futurism in Italy vehemently embraced the rapidly changing forces of modern technological invention, even in its most violent iterations, such as the war machines of the First World War that saw the death of many key members in the group. Yet, as Benjamin Noys informs us, "Futurism isn't simply the celebration of technology and war, but a reworking or struggle to push acceleration into new forms."[2] Such an approach runs counter to virtually all other manifestations of the avant-gardes, most of which follow in the Marxist tradition of resisting consumer capitalism and its demands for the submission of all aspects of life to the maximization of profit (as progress), facilitated by the exploitation of various forms of labor. The Futurists opposed any resistance to the productive forces made possible through the excesses of capitalism, embracing the technologies of ever-fast and ever-newer forms of dynamic creation that they believed could allow them to escape the domination of tradition and history. The question of futurity, central to this *push*, is couched within a particular notion of dynamism that is at the heart of their desire for accelerationism.

Duchamp generally shared this celebration of the machine and machinic qualities as enactments of a modernizing impulse, as well as its role in accelerating the human. In less aggressive and more conceptual ways than the Futurists, he explored the potential of this machinic impulse in a number of his major works. We see it in his painting *Nude Descending a Staircase, No. 2* (1912), in which the photographic camera's indifference, its lack, is an act of capture – capturing static movements. And again in his unfinished – infinitely delayed – *The Bride Stripped Bare by Her Bachelors, Even* or *The Large Glass* (1923), where erotic and sexual patters or redundancies as translated (transmuted) into a machinic visual language, a desiring machine captured as a delay in glass. Duchamp writes in a note from his "Green Box":

> Use 'delay' instead of picture or painting; picture on glass becomes delay in glass – but delay in glass does not mean picture on glass –
>
> It's merely a way of succeeding in no longer thinking that the thing in question is a picture – to make a delay of it in the most general way possible, not so much in the different meanings in which delay can be taken, but rather in their indecisive reunion 'delay' – /a delay in glass as you would say a poem in prose or a spitoon in silver.[3]

This proposed subtitle to *The Large Glass* describes a core element of Duchamp's relationship with the machinic, which necessarily involves moments of lack – hiatuses and ruptures that delay the possibility of fulfillment.

Duchamp was openly critical of the overall project of Futurism. He described the movement as "an impressionism of the mechanical world. It was strictly a continuation of the Impressionist Movement. I was not interested in that. I wanted to get away from the physical aspect of painting."[4] Unlike the Futurists, he understood the prerogative of speeding up culture as an experience of the mind first, before it can be a sensual one – a program that defines the core of the readymade aesthetic. He sees the machine as, in Jean-François Lyotard's works,

> neither and instrument nor a weapon, but an artifice, which is and which is not coupled with nature: it is so coupled in that it does not work without capturing and exploiting natural forces; it is not so coupled in that it plays *a trick* on those forces, being itself less strong than they are, and making real this monstrosity: that the less strong should be stronger than what is stronger.[5]

Unlike the Futurists, Duchamp was aware that the quest to speed up culture would not end with the realization (production) of the dynamic sensation itself, but rather an accelerationist approach could only end with experiential lack, with moments of delay, with boredom – futurity as the boredom of delay. If art represents the ideal of what it means to be human after the Enlightenment, the treasure-trove of modernist ontologies, Duchamp wants to situate this understanding, grounded as it is in futurity (Hegel made sure of this), within the larger questions of art's restlessness in the 20th century – which is now our 21st-century restlessness. Not just the art object but objects more generally seem restless in this age of accelerated experience, in the face of what Patricia MacCormack calls *cosmogenic acceleration*: a model of "time which sees objects in space abandon their centrality to become sources of intensity in duration."[6] Even the object of the body is susceptible to such pressures; as Michael E. Gardiner notes,

> We do not yet know what a technosocial accelerationist body can do, but it will probably involve a lot of sitting around in front of computer monitors, with all the endemic boredom, eye-strain, and lower back pain that entails, stretching into any conceivable future.[7]

This is the object's lack, its boredom – with us, even with itself. If the object can be said to *stare back* it is with bored disbelief.

Resting on its pedestal, Duchamp's *Bottle Rack* looks to us, its viewers, for a meaning it cannot hold or possess but instead is happy to – not reflect – refract back onto us (although there is always a delay). It sits there indifferent, a moment of intensity in the extended duration of its boredom that modulates the parameters of a readymade aesthetic. Guattari will base his ethico-aesthetic paradigm in part on such an understanding of the readymade, not primarily as an artistic but rather a philosophical gesture, which allows for interpretations beyond the *given* structures of modern subjectivity towards what he describes as "a constellation of Universes."[8] Within this cosmology the readymade becomes the black hole function, an accelerated absence or delay or gap that invites onlookers to self-consciously recognize the exchanges of values taking place around this (indifferent) object. The readymade creates meaning and value not directly but rather in the repeated and repeatable interpretive delay between the commodity object and the art object.

"Focusing on things that are exchanged, rather than simply on the forms or function of exchange," Arjun Appadurai writes, "makes it possible to argue that what creates the link between exchange and value is *politics*, constructed broadly."[9] The politics of the Duchampian readymade are therefore quite relevant to questioning this process of object-oriented valuation on the level of subjective experience, especially considerations of how individuals create identity through the meanings given to objects. Yet the moment the object ceases to be 'object', what does it become? When a couch or iPad or reproduction of an artwork fails to be the object it is, its constitution either shifts, becoming another form of model (garbage, waste, pastness) or is reconceived as multiple (parts, pieces, fragments). It becomes a gap, a black hole function – bored futurity. And Duchamp will famously claim that art is this *gap*, with the meaning of an artwork being contained within the lack separating self from object, the black hole that is also the container of subjective valuations.

Notes

1 Gilles Deleuze and Felix Guattari, *A Thousand Plateaus: Capitalism and Schizophrenia*, trans. Brian Massumi (Minneapolis: University of Minnesota Press, 2005), 40; 167.
2 Benjamin Noys, *Malign Velocities: Accelerationism and Capitalism* (Winchester: Zero Books, 2014), 17.
3 Marcel Duchamp, "The Green Box," *The Writings of Marcel Duchamp*, eds. Michel Sanouillet and Elmer Peterson (New York: Da Capo, 1973), 26. Joselit will make an interesting observation in relation to this note, connecting Duchamp's ideas of delay (or *deferral*) to "both desire and the shop window," in which the "membrane of the glass brings the commodity into being by establishing a paradoxical relationship of proximity and distance that produces desire in the viewer/consumer." Joselit, *Infinite Regress*, 143–144.
4 Marcel Duchamp, "The Great Trouble with Art in This Country," *The Writings of Marcel Duchamp*, eds. Michel Sanouillet and Elmer Peterson (New York: Da Capo, 1973), 125.
5 Lyotard, *Duchamp's TRANS/formers*, 42. It is worth remembering Roberto Esposito's claim that "technology is not necessarily opposed to nature; in fact, as far as our species is concerned, technology is the fruit of our nature." Esposito, *Persons and Things*, 118.
6 Patricia MacCormack, "Cosmogenic Acceleration: Futurity and Ethics," *e-flux journal* 46 (June 2013): www.e-flux.com.
7 Michael E. Gardiner, "Critique of Accelerationism," *Theory, Culture & Society* 34.1 (2017): 49.
8 Félix Guattari, *Chaosmosis, An Ethico-Aesthetic Paradigm*, trans. Paul Bains and Julian Pefanis (Bloomington: Indiana University Press, 1995), 17.
9 Arjun Appadurai, Introduction, in *The Social Life of Things: Commodities in Cultural Perspective* (Cambridge: Cambridge University Press 1996), 3.

11 Consequences of a Duchampian accelerationism [2]

The second consequence of a Duchampian form of accelerationist aesthetics is the need to recognize the object, not as the source or origin but rather the black hole of subjection, a process the readymade actively speeds up. What we experience when encountering a readymade is not the object itself but rather the accelerated experiences that surround it, that frame it: from the museum and its museological accoutrements, to the history of art in which it is situated and to which it must necessarily speak, to our own reception of the object, our interpretation of its *inner qualifications* (as Duchamp says). It therefore plays upon and extends to the point of absurdity the manner in which modern historicizations of art act to capture all other 'art' that comes *within its reach*, those objects created at different times and in different cultures that were never intended to be 'art' but are now nonetheless housed within the books of art history; a process in modernity that is now used to produce any object within (or as) 'history'.

The often repeated question raised by the readymade – *is it art?* – is symptomatic of its enactment of the frame of 'art' without actually providing a viable object to support or corroborate this framework. A large part of art's privileged status comes from the fact that its objects are understood as decidedly unique and culturally special. Historically, this is related to the talent required to produce such objects – think here of Leonardo da Vinci's *Mona Lisa* and Rachel Ruysch's still-lifes – but also, especially within modernity, because the art object maintains a vital ideal of humanity. As Peter Bürger states:

> The citizen who, in everyday life, has been reduced to a partial function (*means–ends activity*) can be discovered in art as a 'human being'. Here, one can unfold the abundance of one's talents, though with the proviso that this sphere remain strictly separate from the praxis of life.[1]

Duchamp breaks this cardinal rule with the readymade. (It is often argued that Cubist collage broke this division of spheres, Bürger being a key proponent of this theory; I disagree since the Cubists' use of everyday material did not fundamentally challenge the space of art, but instead simply used these 'reality' fragments to continue making what were art objects.) By bringing objects from everyday life into the idealized realm of art Duchamp insinuates the question of *means–ends activity* into the relationship of art and objects, while also suggesting that the quest to be discovered as *human being* is not restricted to the art object but instead can include critical treatments of objects in general – a hypothesis that the Surrealists will extensively develop through a exploration of what Walter Benjamin calls *profane illumination*.

Kojin Karatani discusses Duchamp's practice in terms of what he calls 'bracketing', which actively focuses on specific experiences of an object while ignoring or putting aside others; "with Kant it became clear that what makes art art is the subjective act of bracketing other concerns," which Karatani will explicitly state connects art to commodification.[2] We can see that a critical approach to art requires not just that such acts of bracketing be made conscious and visible but also that we remember, at crucial moments of experience and historicization, to *unbracket* our experiences – to allow the ethical, political and economic concerns to become part of our personal interpretations and judgments.

While the roots of this assessment are to be found in Kant's notion of the aesthetic, the actualization of such a perspective is announced in and through Duchamp's readymade aesthetic and its overt challenge to the central conception of the art object under modernity. Also, there is the centering principle of the artist, who is authoritatively outside and precedes this object –yet believes the object historically points to them. The nature of the readymade, its focus on the lack of singularity and total submission to the logic of simulation, is such that it functions through a self-conscious recognition of an accelerated subjective judgment.

When we stand in front of a painting by Johannes Vermeer or Pablo Picasso, to choose but two examples, we assume attributes onto the object of the painting (equal to 'art'), which therefore does not raise questions about the possibility of such a framing or bracketing. These encounters are enacted in what may be considered a pre-Kantian understanding of the aesthetic, by which I mean that the experience of the painting assumes the beauty (meaning) of the work to be an actual part of its material constitution. It just *is* beautiful (meaningful) and anyone who does not see this beauty (meaning) in the work is simply wrong, must look more closely, must learn to see it – which means, of course, to see it from a particular cultural and historical perspective, often Eurocentric. When Kant argues for an aesthetic that is purely subjective, referring to the subject of the representation, not the object that is the thing of the representation, he removes the experience from the domain of the object and places it firmly within that of the subject, locating meaning within the realm of subjectivity. If a painting is beautiful (meaningful) it is so because that is the way it is perceived and interpreted, a judgment that can and often does change over time. Duchamp will define this as its posterity. The same can be said about the readymade, the beauty or ugliness (or boredom) of which is not considered part of the object, not a reality to be experienced but rather is integral to its reception, to the specific act of experience embodied by the spectator. It is the spectator who must create the meaning of the object – which, it must be remembered, necessarily involves choosing whether it is an art object or not. I will even go so far as to say that in terms of the readymade, the actual object is virtually irrelevant: it is a black hole defined through inherent interpretations or meanings, the actual experience of which is projected onto this *indifferent* object. The fact that one urinal can be replaced by another and still be *Fountain*, or the broken glass ampoule of *Paris Air* can be replaced by another and be considered simply 'broken and later restored' demonstrates this point.

This is the true challenge of the readymade and the core of Duchampian accelerationism: the manner in which, when engaging with objects in modernity, subjective interpretations are mistaken as objective qualities that we 'see' *in* things. The meaning that I experience in relation to the objects I choose and accept in my life may be subjective, but such objects become interpretable qualities of my existence as subject; this is how the choice economy controls the parameters of subjectivity. If objects within advanced consumer capitalism are no longer tied to questions of use or personal freedom, the act of choosing (purchasing) is now a veritable burden masked by desire, in which choice only begets the necessity for more choice as one is forced to contend with the infinite regression of the logic of simulation. The individual purchasing and re-purchasing objects is, through this act, perpetually re-enacting the materialization of their own subjectivity in and through each object chosen and re-chosen, a process that makes subjective meaning appear as an objective quality that can be perceived and communicated with others (objects act as bracketing devices that frame our public sense of self).

Yet the meanings that I interpret into the experience of my couch or my computer are not qualities of the object and are not perceivable to someone who does not know me. Reciprocally, the reproduced winter landscapes *not* chosen by Duchamp are equally meaningless in relation to his practice as the ones he (randomly) picked up and used as *Pharmacy*. The object's acts of interpellation are in fact related to subjective judgments that we do not recognize as such, instead responding as if the object held authority over the possibility of experiencing meaning in the world. As if, without the hail of the object, a cornerstone of consumerist discourse, meaning is not possible.

The readymade uses this process to enact an event of meaningfulness by presenting an object that is purposefully non-authoritative in itself, the presence of which fails to give meaning to spectators unless they are willing to creatively see such *meaning* for themselves, see the object as art. He does help us with this leap of *artistic faith*, embedding the work into the external discourse of the museum and art history more generally; "you accepted the idea that *your* entire work would be in a museum?" Pierre Cabanne asks Duchamp, to which he responds: "I accepted because there are practical things in life that one can't stop. I wasn't going to refuse. I could have torn them up or broken them; that would have been an idiotic gesture."[3] Actively locating his 'art' objects within the environment of the museum, he chose to place them inside one of the quintessential bracketing institutions of modernity (of the Enlightenment), with its vast white – even when they are not white – walls, plain plinths, exhibitionary display cases and, of course, informational tags or placards. Far from simply accepting this fate, many believe Duchamp choreographed this final artistic resting place to facilitate future meanings and histories for his works.

Duchamp's often mischievous engagements with the language of curation and art history are well known. Take as an example his treatment of the urinal and/or *Fountain* after it failed to be exhibited in the April 1917 Society of Independent Artists exhibition. Before the urinal was put aside or discarded, Duchamp, with the help of Beatrice Wood, took the object to the studio of noted American photographer Alfred Stieglitz, who agreed to photograph it. "He took great pains with the lighting, and did it with such skill that a shadow fell across the urinal suggesting a veil," Wood recounts.[4] Stieglitz's choice to stage and photograph the urinal as he did – set off-centered on a plinth, pictured so that the base of Fountain (with its black hole) is in the middle of the image, posed in front of the sympathetic undulating forms of the painter Marsden Hartley's *The Warriors* – represented his creative act of viewing this everyday object as art, giving it meaning through this process that it did not have previously. Not a mere document of the object or art object, Duchamp's attentiveness to this moment of historicization, the moment in which a urinal is transformed through Stieglitz's famous photograph into Fountain, points to his understanding of history as untimely ready-made events.

While Duchamp helps us with our leap of artistic faith, through indifference more than anything else, he strategically leaves it to us, the object's onlookers, to make (and re-make) the final choice. Only we can pass the final judgment on the object. Only we can bring the work into contact with the world, make it part of lived experience in the specific time and place in which we exist – the work's futurity. Only we, through layers of interpretations, can give a work of art its posterity by creating and re-creating its meanings with each new spatial and temporal rethinking of this object.

It may again be observed that this argument can be applied to the experience of any work by any artist: that is Duchamp's point. The readymade is not a departure from the reality of art conceived and practiced under modernity. Instead, it is an acceleration of its aesthetic and ontological qualities, of its calling the subject to witness the creation of its own subjectivity. Similarly, the ability of the readymade to mimic everyday relations with objects under consumerism is less a point of distinction, as is commonly understood, and more a material exaggeration of art's inevitable dependence on the language of capitalist modes of production and forms of logic. The assumed givenness of meaning within the particular model of consumer capitalism is of special interest to Duchamp, who wants to demonstrate the other side of this particular conception and practice of the object that must interpellate its subject, in which the object becomes a black hole of modern subjection that depends upon the subject's effectual engagements for its actualization. We can therefore speak to this condition beyond the readymade proper, beyond the production of mere objects, understanding this aesthetic as an alternative discourse for thinking object-oriented – Guy Debord might say *image*-oriented – relationships within in our era of late capitalism.

Notes

1 Bürger, *Theory of the Avant-Garde*, 48–49.
2 Kojin Karatani, "Uses of Aesthetics after Orientalism," trans. Sabu Kohso, *Boundary 2* 25.2 (1998): 150.
3 Marcel Duchamp to Pierre Cabanne, *Dialogues with Marcel Duchamp*, trans. Ron Padgett (New York: Da Capo Press, 1987), 71.
4 Beatrice Wood, "I Shock Myself [extracts]," in *3 New York Dadas and the Blind Man* (London: Atlas Press, 2013), 165.

12 *Tzanck Check*

Confronted with *Tzanck Check* (1919) (see Figure 10) it is difficult not to see the broader implications of Duchamp's readymade practice, particularly within modern industrial and post-industrial culture. As a work it sits comfortably within the overlapping discourses of art and economics, always reminding the interested (artistically invested) viewer of the monetarily interested (financially invested) qualities inherent in the treatment of the art object within modernity. If an avant-gardist aesthetic is about defining a sphere of life that escapes being measured in terms of the reductive demands of profitability, it is the functioning of economics that such a perspective attempts to resist. This is a world in which creative and intellectual endeavours are constantly interrupted by the needs and desires of everyday living, real and imagined; each demands varying levels of remuneration, which in turn means that we must have currency, money or otherwise, to pay for these needs and desires. Going to the dentist to take care of one's teeth, a form of basic bodily maintenance, requires one to pay for these dental services; in one case Duchamp paid his dentist, Daniel Tzanck, with an imitation cheque made out in the amount of $115, exactly what he would have owed if he paid in monetary currency.

The work exists, in principle, as both art object and object. Tzanck obviously accepted this in place of a monetary payment because of the object's privileged status as 'art' – many poets and painters became his patients because of "his willingness to be paid in kind with books, drawings and other works."[1] But, unlike the other artworks Tzanck acquired in this manner, Duchamp's has the unique apparition of the financial qualities that are at the root of this exchange. *Tzanck Check* mimics precisely the visual characteristics of a personal cheque, a modern bill of exchange between two individuals or parties. Through this written/textual order one party – *Marcel Duchamp* – instructs a bank – *The Teeth's Loan and Trust Company Consolidated* – to pay a certain sum – *one hundred fifteen and no/100 dollars* – to the party addressed (hailed) by the object – *Daniel Tzanck*. Although the actual object

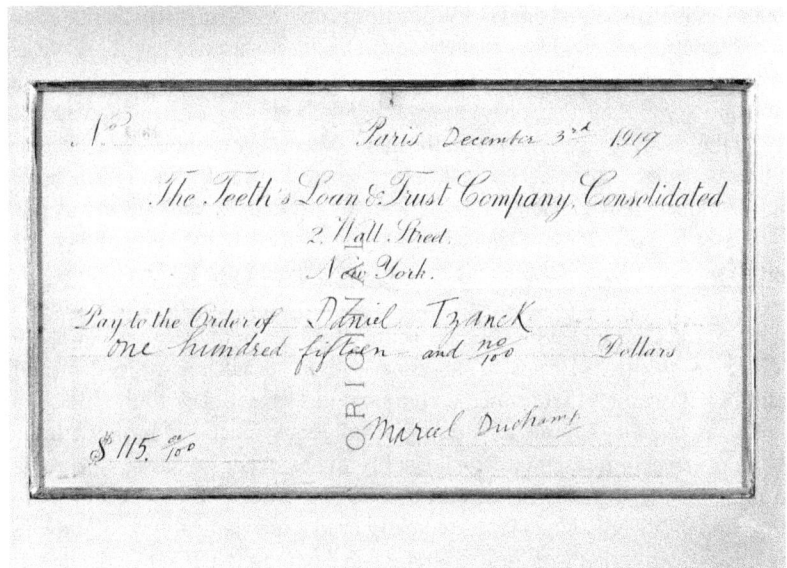

Figure 10 Marcel Duchamp, *Tzanck Check*, 1919. Ink on paper. 21 x 38.2 cm. The Vera and Arturo Schwarz Collection of Dada and Surrealist Art in the Israel Museum © Association Marcel Duchamp / ADAGP, Paris / SOCAN, Montreal (2019).

Photo © The Israel Museum Jerusalem by Avshalom Avital.

of the cheque is oversized, virtually all the other details reflect the general appearance of an authentic personal cheque that is mechanically printed and sequentially numbered – this one is *no. 4864* – with lines provided to write in the specific information of a given exchange. As a symbolic object of exchange, this cheque must be understood not as a fake or forgery but rather, to borrow readymade terminology, as authentic-aided.

Duchamp does not make a cheque that is meant to fool people into believing it is real, but rather creates a simulated cheque by hand that celebrates its contradictory status as document – which, especially in person, is quite compelling. Most interesting are the apparently printed elements that are in actuality hand drawn, such as the numbering of the cheque and the word *ORIGINAL* vertically traversing the center of the sheet; the fine rows of text spelling out the faux-bank's name (without spaces) that form a repeating pattern across the lower half of the paper, similar to a watermark, are said to be produced using a rubber stamp made by the artist for this work. "I took a long time doing the little letters, to do something which would look printed – it wasn't a small check," Duchamp informs us.[2] (Are the apparently stamped letters in fact also hand drawn?) While this is obviously an artistic simulation, it did function exactly like a real cheque in that it was used to pay for services. The signature across the bottom bridges these two contradictory states: giving authenticity to the (imaginary) transfer of funds on the one hand and authorizing the artwork (as payment) on the other. Necessary for both is the declaration of *original*, literal in this case, a privileged status that allows the receiver of the object, be it a cheque and/or a work of art, to trust in its claim to value.

Described as a drawing (ink on paper), the institutional quality of the overall design of *Tzanck Check* was thoroughly planned out by Duchamp, as is evident from the sketch he made in preparation for the work. This was not a frivolous act but instead involved careful planning and clear sense of detail. There are wonderful folds in the paper – as if it had been folded in half, and in half again – that immediately refers this object back to the life of an everyday cheque that one puts in one's wallet or pocket. Balanced with this is an overwhelmingly impersonal quality to the overall work as document, a bureaucratic impulse Elena Filipovic claims Duchamp used consistently throughout his practice.[3] He strategically used a mechanical type of drawing to create a work that gets away from personal expression, that avoids the trap of taste: "good or bad, it's the same thing, it's still taste."[4]

Beginning with his painting *Coffee Mill* (1911) we see the use of the machinic as an alternative to personal taste, which he believed to be a limiting factor in art, since taste was based merely on personal (momentary) likes and dislikes. He used the machinic as a language that appeared neutral, with *no taste*, such as with the diagrammatic elements describing the movement of the coffee mill or the apparently printed text in *Tzanck Check*. "Duchamp, I think single-handedly, demonstrated that it is entirely possible for something to be art without having anything to do with taste at all, good or bad," which Arthur C. Danto will see as the end of "the era of taste" and the beginning of "the era of meaning. The question is not whether something is in good or bad taste, but what does it mean."[5] This strategy is epitomized in the readymades.

> The difference between Duchamp's enterprise and the Cubists' earlier one lies in his clear cut determination to cut short any counterattack of taste. He did not select a bicycle wheel as a beautiful modern object, as a Futurist might; he chose it just because it was *commonplace*. It was nothing but a wheel, like a hundred others, and in fact if it were lost it could soon be replaced by identical 'replicas'.[6]

The readymades extend the refusal of taste to an extreme in the form of purely mechanical and reproducible objects that reduce the personal to pre-existing and already-made parameters.

It is this overlap that situates *Tzanck Check* within an extended understanding of the readymade aesthetic. Although it is not a pre-existing object, and it is produced by the artist's hand, the work nonetheless is fundamentally based on the readymade structure and form of a personal cheque; Duchamp did not create but instead chose the object of this document, which he methodically imitated. The fact is he made by hand an object that could be – that he could have – mechanically produced.

Tzanck Check is a simulation of this (at the time) everyday object, which directly references issues of personal finance and an individual's relationship with existing economic realities. More importantly, it defines a moment of interpersonal exchange. In this case, the cheque represents a financial exchange between Duchamp and Tzanck, with the object being at one and the same time used as payment for the latter's dental services and created as a document of this exchange; such a process was extended when, years later, Duchamp purchased the cheque back from Tzanck for more than the amount noted on the work (readymade inflation). Treated as a readymade model, the extension of the work continued through new iterations of this model: reproduced in the first issue of Francis Picabia's journal *Cannibale*, reproduced full-scale as part of Duchamp's *Boîte-en-valise* (self-contained and self-referential futurity). For Duchamp the exchange and exchangeability of values define the economy of art within modern culture – Georg Simmel in *The Philosophy of Money* will claim "value is in a sense the counterpoint to being, and is comparable to being as a comprehensive form and category of the world view."[7] At its base, *Tzanck Check* focuses on the question of value, not just in terms of objects (cheques, money) but also and more importantly the relationships among people that are mediated through such objects.

Notes

1 Peter Read, "The *Tzanck Check* and Related Works by Marcel Duchamp," in *Marcel Duchamp: Artist of the Century,* eds. Rudolf Kuenzli and Francis M. Naumann (Cambridge: MIT Press, 1989), 96.

2 Duchamp to Cabanne, *Dialogues with Marcel Duchamp*, 63.

3 See Elena Filipovic, *The Apparently Marginal Activities of Marcel Duchamp* (Cambridge: MIT Press, 2016), 21.

4 Duchamp to Cabanne, *Dialogues with Marcel Duchamp*, 48.

5 Arthur C. Danto, "Marcel Duchamp and the End of Taste: A Defense of Contemporary Art," *Tout-Fait: The Marcel Duchamp Studies Online Journal* (2016): www.toutfait.com/articals.

6 Robert Lebel, *Marcel Duchamp*, trans. George Heard Hamilton (New York: Grove Press, 1959), 35.

7 Georg Simmel, *The Philosophy of Money* (London: Routledge, 2011), 62.

13 Note on a readymade economics

Readymade economics are defined through a notion of the object as relationship. If "economics is the study of human behavior, with a particular focus on human decision making,"[1] we can understand readymade economics as the study of already-existing social and cultural relations that individuals choose from (choice economy), with a focus on objects as mediators of these subjective relationships.

Choices, as well as the mechanisms through which decisions are made within the socio-political realities of advanced consumer capitalism, are tied fundamentally to the question of value and its connection to subjective judgment. The study of human behavior is in a way an examination of systems of human valuations, what Simmel terms the subjectivity of value that cannot be defined yet gives meaning to our lived experiences. Money economies attempt to give value a material existence, but this is merely a symbolic gesture that has no basis in the reality of subjective value as consciousness. In fact, Simmel stresses, "value is not attached to objects in the same way as is colour or temperature," and we must recognize that "the two series constituted by reality and by value are quite independent of each other."[2] Extending Duchamp's readymade mode of production into the realm of economics allows us to propose a system of valuations that takes seriously the intrinsically subjective nature of this conflict, positing the problematics of economies as internal to individual experiences or, in a true sense, co-creations of such values.

In terms of the readymade as an aesthetic practice, value is presented in a state of contradiction, a 'counderstanding' of opposites that must be reconciled by each spectator individually. Such values are not merely given or present but must instead be constantly created and re-created with each (repeatable) moment of effectual realization. It is not enough to view *Fountain* or *Tzanck Check* and decide it is art, you must make and re-make this decision on each occasion with the object – with the knowledge that you may in certain moments choose differently. With most works of art this perpetual choice is obscured by the givenness of decision-making mechanisms, such as the museum and art history, which enable us to assume value onto an object without actually judging it for ourselves. Because the readymade is non-originary and imminently repeatable, always already replaced by another from the series, it is the instant of maximum conflict between reality and value. The ecology of the readymade's exchangeability is vital to understanding how it functions and, in a true sense, its economy of judgments. We can reword this as an impossible aesthetic and even political question: when is the object 'art' and when is it not?

Duchamp's "interest in economics is conceptual," writes Dalia Judovitz, "it involves understanding the mechanisms involved in the generation and expenditure of value."[3] This interest is seen most obviously in his financial-themed works; in addition to *Tzanck Check* the main examples include *Check Bruno* (1965), *Check Czech* (1965) and *Monte Carlo Bond* (1924), all of which enact exchanges that bring into conflict economic and artistic values. Beyond this conflict there is the economics of the readymade aesthetic, a logic that permeates Duchamp's entire practice and philosophy of art.

The possibility of a readymade economics reflects his larger belief in the power of an individual's ability to subjectively judge, which necessarily includes the courage and freedom to use one's own faculty of judgment. Byung-Chul Han talks about such freedom in terms of the *should* and the *can*. "The freedom of *Can* generates even more coercion than the disciplinarian *Should*, which issues commandments and prohibitions. *Should* has a limit. In contrast, *Can* has none. Thus, the compulsion entitled by *Can* is unlimited."[4] Much of the development of the idea of the readymade after Duchamp participates in exploring the *can* – can a given object be art? And the answer is always yes, feeding into the limitless compulsion that has become a consumerist mode of understanding art. For Duchamp the readymade aesthetic operates through the necessities of the *should* – should this object be art, in this time and in this place? This is *hinge logic*, the "pass from the 'it's possible' to the 'it's necessary'."[5] Readymade economics locates value strictly in the necessities of the *should* that is the expenditure of true and effectual individual judgment.

Notes

1 James D. Gwartney et al., *Economics: Private and Public Choice*, 12th edition (Mason: Thomson, 2008), 3.
2 Simmel, *The Philosophy of Money*, 65.
3 Dalia Judovitz, "Art and Economics: Duchamp's Postmodern Returns," *Criticism* 35.2 (Spring 1993): 215.
4 Byung-Chul Han, *Psychopolitics: Neoliberalism and New Technologies of Power*, trans. Erik Butler (London: Verso, 2017), 1–2.
5 Lyotard, *Duchamp's TRANS/formers*, 119.

14 Missed creative acts

Readymade aesthetics depend upon the possibility of failure, the possibility that the creative act can and does fail. One of the core problematics that emerge out of modern historicizations of art is the reluctance and even refusal to experience those moments when an object is unable to hail or interpellate its subject. Can any of us honestly say that every time we set eyes on a celebrated work of art it calls to us? That there are not times when we experience nothing? When the *Mona Lisa* is just a small painting with lots of people crowded around it?

We can formulate this in terms of our experience of the creative act as a missed experience,[1] in which the possibilities of encountering the art object are defined through a futurity that is the lost possibility of creating meaning. As spectators we exceed, surpass and supress an experience we never experienced – sensing a loss in the event of art that questions the foundation of our relationship with these objects of 'art', a lack that cannot be blamed on the artist or artwork alone. Our role in this missed experience must be acknowledged. To put this in Duchampian terms:

> All in all, the failure of the creative act is not performed by the artist alone; it is the spectator who fails to bring the work in contact with the external world by being unable to decipher and interpret its inner qualifications and thus does not add their contribution to this missed creative act.

The question of posterity, which is central to Duchamp's formulation of the creative act, demands a consideration of not only the possibility of an art object being understood and appreciated as meaningful in a future place and time, but equally knowing the inherent impossibility of such meaning always being present or the same.

The profound cultural and historical meanings we (in the early 21st century) ascribe to Leonardo da Vinci's portrait of – apparently – Lisa

Gherardini have no relation to the painting's purpose and meaning(s) when it was painted, for the artist or those who had a relationship to the work. In fact, we could even go so far as to say that our experience is a missed experience of the *Mona Lisa* because we fail to *decipher and interpret* the work painted and understood in the Renaissance, instead projecting our own (futurated) vision of its *inner qualifications* onto the already passed object of the painting. As Duchamp says, "Don't let yourself become hypnotized by the smiles of yesterday; rather invent the smiles of tomorrow."[2]

Is *L.H.O.O.Q.* (1919) Duchamp's creative acknowledgment of his own failure as a spectator to complete the creative act started by Leonardo da Vinci? Is it his boredom with the *Mona Lisa* as 'art'?

This process speeds up within the readymade mode of production, which in most cases entails a double failure of the object. On the one hand, the artist fails to recognize the object for what it is, for the purposes and use-values (or values of use) that define its production and distribution. In his act of putting a urinal on display within an artistic context, Duchamp fails to recognize the object's purposive existence as a lavatory feature for a men's washroom that is meant to be urinated in. On the other hand, the spectator's acceptance of this failure by also failing to recognize the object's purposive function and believing it to be 'art' compounds the issue. We must never forget that it is we, the viewers of this urinal, who actually turn (and continually re-turn) the object into the art object *Fountain*.

Such a double failure highlights the manner in which the readymades push to the point of excess the discourse of art as a core practice of modernity. "By 'modernity' I mean the ephemeral, the fugitive, the contingent, the other half of the eternal and immutable," Charles Baudelaire writes.[3] The readymade clearly exaggerates the contingent nature of modernity – especially T. J. Clark's sense of contingency as "turning from past to future, the acceptance of risk, the omnipresence of change, the malleability of time and space," all of which are integral to the readymade aesthetic.[4] Yet is there not also a hint of the *eternal and immutable* in the practice of the readymade, something suspiciously like Plato's realm of the forms? Each object chosen, a snow shovel for example, exists for us as a (repeatable and reproducible) shadow of an idea of the *real* readymade, *In Advance of the Broken Arm*. The readymade takes this directly from the realities of consumer objects in advanced capitalism, which continually fail to live up to the missed realities of their non-existent 'original' (hyperreal) form. In Baudrillardian terms, this is the simulacra of simulation; in Duchamp's words, the "apparition of an appearance."[5]

The readymade fails to be a moment of the eternal and immutable (as consumerist production), but the possibility – the possible *should* – appears to remain imminently present. This reciprocally betrays the overarching sense of its contingency as well, which is pushed to its most extreme aesthetic point: the readymade is the moment when the past becomes an absent futurity made presence through this all too visible lack. And Duchamp's alter ego Rrose Sélavy becomes the trickster figure, or a *trickster signature* in Gerald Vizenor's terms[6] – since it is Rrose who authorizes much of Duchamp's later artistic practices, appearing as solo or collaborative signatory – who enacts and personifies this double failure by continually pointing out the presence of the immanent gap of 'art'.

From this perspective, we must rethink the infamous tale of the museum custodian who mistook Duchamp's *In Advance of the Broken Arm* for a mere snow shovel, using the object to actually shovel snow.[7] While it remains true that the custodian failed to recognize the object as a work of art, what is overlooked is the reciprocal failure of those from the art world (museum staff, visitors, art critics and historians) who did not see the object as a functional shovel. This dual failure is the complete experience of the readymade. At each moment the readymade must exist potentially as mere object and/or art object – a decision and judgment powerfully relegated to each and every spectator that stands in front of the work.

Let us stress this point: every experience is also a missed experience, since one cannot experience the object and the art object together, simultaneously. Like an optical illusion – of which Duchamp was particularly fond – at any given moment the snow shovel can be *In Advance of the Broken Arm* or just a snow shovel, the urinal can be *Fountain* or just another urinal. This split state, this schizophrenic identity of art under modernity, is hailed by the Duchampian readymade aesthetic.

For Baudrillard, I would hypothesize, the logic of simulation is grounded in hyperreal – *infrathin* – interpretations that constantly negotiate between experience and missed experience, meanings found as much as meanings lost (personal interests and personal boredoms). How else can we explain the gap of subjective experience except as that which at times we fulfill and at others we fall into, captured by the gravity of the occluded meanings that seize us through our historical and historicizing proximity to the object. In this way, we can see the failure of *Fountain* (or any readymade) as the foundation for its greater success.

Notes

1 This line of thinking is indebted to Rebecca Comay's book *Mourning Sickness: Hegel and the French Revolution* (Stanford: Stanford University Press, 2010).
2 Duchamp, quoted in H. P. Roché, "Souvenirs of Marcel Duchamp," in Robert Lebel, *Marcel Duchamp*, trans. George Heard Hamilton (New York: Grove Press, 1959), 87.
3 Charles Baudelaire, "The Painter of Modern Life," in *The Painter of Modern Life and Other Essays*, trans. Jonathan Mayne (London: Phaidon Press, 2010), 12.

4 T. J. Clark, *Farwell to an Idea* (New Haven: Yale University Press, 2014), 10.
5 Duchamp, *Marcel Duchamp, Notes*, np. See note 250.
6 Discussed as a "postmodern condition in the critical responses to Native American Indian literatures," Vizenor describes the trickster signature as "an uncertain humor that denies translation and tribal representations." Gerald Vizenor, Preface, *Narrative Chance: Postmodern Discourse on Native American Indian Literatures*, ed. Gerald Vizenor (Norman: University of Oklahoma Press, 1993), ix.
7 One version of this story is told by George Heard Hamilton in his 1966 essay "In Advance of the Broken Arm?" reprinted in *Marcel Duchamp in Perspective*, ed. Joseph Masheck (New York: Da Capo Press, 2002), 74.

15 Remade readymades

Duchamp was well aware of the inherent double failure at the heart of the readymade aesthetic. So too was he aware of the success made possible through the contradictions of such *infrathin* failures, which define the economy of Duchampian accelerationism. We see this when he commended the museum custodian for using *In Advance of the Broken Arm* to shovel snow. And when he allowed (so-called) facsimiles of his readymades to be exhibited as *his* readymades, such as the urinal Sidney Janis used as *Fountain* in 1950, the version of *3 Standard Stoppages* (1913–1914) Walter Hopps had made for the 1963 *Duchamp* Retrospective at the Pasadena Art Museum and Ulf Linde's versions of *Bicycle Wheel*, which Duchamp inscribed retroactively – after it was exhibited – as '*copie conforme*' or 'certified true copy'. And again when he, after repeatedly proclaiming that he never sold a readymade, agreed to allow Arturo Schwarz in 1964 to produce and sell editions of the main readymades.

What made Schwarz's venture different from previous remakings (resubstantiations) was the "fanatical care" he took in creating versions that as closely as possible resembled the models of the first objects Duchamp chose (see Figure 11). "The *Bicycle Wheel* for instance is not any bicycle wheel which would have a curved fork. Schwarz took great pains in having it made straight after the old photograph," Duchamp tells Robert Lebel, "I busied myself with this edition to the point of 'press-proofing' each item. I oversaw them you see."[1] This required Schwarz not simply to purchase a number of ready-made objects, as most had done in the past, now impractical given the numbers needed, but rather to manufacture an edition of objects that perform the models of the first readymades.

To accomplish this task, professionally engineered blueprints were drafted for each readymade, with extreme attention to detail. These were based on photographs of the readymades and, for those still in existence, descriptive information from museums on the material make-up of the object(s). Duchamp went over each blueprint for each readymade noting corrections

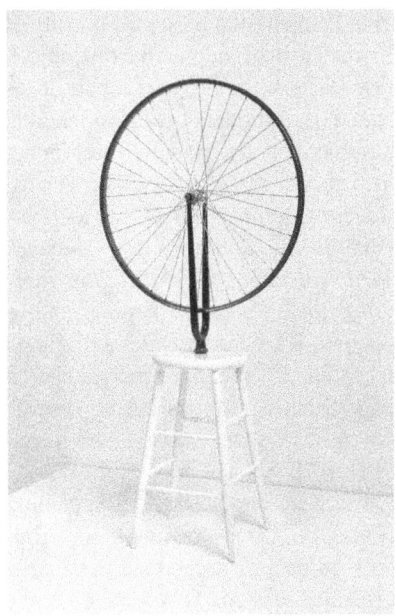

Figure 11 Marcel Duchamp, *Bicycle Wheel*, 1964 [replica of 1913 original]. Bicycle fork and wheel, painted wooden stool. 128.3 × 63.5 × 31.8 cm (50 ½ x 25 x 12 ½ inches). Philadelphia Museum of Art, Gift of the Galleria Schwarz d'Arte, Milan, 1964-175-1 © Association Marcel Duchamp / ADAGP, Paris / SOCAN, Montreal (2019).

Photo courtesy of the Philadelphia Museum of Art.

and, once he was satisfied, he inscribed it with *OK Marcel Duchamp*. Given his interest in mechanical types of drawing, as a way of removing oneself as much as possible from personal taste, one can understand his enthusiasm at overseeing production of these readymades – which, in this case, was the production of the models from which all of the readymade forms in this edition proceed (according to *infrathin* modular differences). Schwarz includes a number of the blueprints in *The Complete Works of Marcel Duchamp*, the entries for all of which begin with a statement in which Duchamp is quoted as saying the drawings might be a "Readymade to the square power."[2] Duchampian accelerationism is seen here as a condition of the model.

It is this obvious crafting of the object, especially with a concern for exactness and fidelity, that many critics felt was against the spirit of critique that marked the readymade mode of artistic production instituted by Duchamp in the 1910s. But the readymade as act focuses not on the past, not on what the object might have meant when it was chosen or to earlier spectators. Instead it is speculative, defining an object-oriented pursuit of a projected futurity of values – determined in and through individual acts of judging the (art)object. (For me, this includes Duchamp's experience of bringing together all of his readymades, of making them into a collection of models.) It is the inherent accelerationist nature of the readymade aesthetic, tied to notions of reproducibility and posterity, which these editioned almost-ready-made objects enact.

Fourteen of Duchamp's readymades were given new (historical and personal) life: *Bicycle Wheel, 3 Standard Stoppages, Bottle Rack, In Advance of the Broken Arm, Comb, With Hidden Noise, Traveler's Folding Item, Apolinère Enameled, Fountain, Trap, Hat Rack, Paris Air, Fresh Window, Why Not Sneeze Rrose Sélavy?* Adina Kamien-Kazhdan provides a thorough accounting of the process that saw each of these (re)produced in a numbered edition of eight plus two proofs, "one for Duchamp (inscribed *ex. Rrose*)" and "one for Schwarz (inscribed: *ex. Arturo*)," as well as "two exhibition copies for museum collections (numbered I/II, II/II, Ex. h.c. pour exposition)."[3] At the time, a number of these readymades were on the verge of becoming mythological, the objects themselves having been long lost; with no 'original' bottle-drying rack, or inscription for that matter – forgotten by the artist himself – all that remained was an idea (ideal) *Bottle Rack*. We can see in the editioned readymades an act of re-embodiment in which each is again manifest within a simultaneously chosen and constructed object.

There is a base contradiction regarding the condition of an object within advanced consumer capitalism that is being played out through these remade readymades, one that Duchamp revels in and around which he constructs his general philosophy of art. When asked about the paradox of this gesture, Duchamp responded by saying:

> There is an absolute contradiction, but that is what is enjoyable, isn't it? Bringing in the idea of contradiction, the notion of contradiction, which is something that has never really been used, you see? And all the more since this use doesn't go very far. If you make an edition of eight Readymades, like a sculpture, like a Bourdelle or you name it, that is not overdoing it. There is something called 'multiples,' that go up to hundred and fifty, two hundred copies. Now there I do object because that's getting really too vulgar in a useless way, with things that could be interesting if they were seen by fewer people.[4]

Of these editioned readymades, *Fountain* was the only one "not produced solely by a craftsman." As Helen Molesworth notes: "A mold was made by a ceramicist and given to an Italian plumbing manufacturer, where, one evening, the factory line of mass production was halted as twelve *Fountain* sculptures were made instead."[5] Limited mass-production (*seen by fewer people*) interrupts *mass*-mass-production in a gesture of acknowledging the need for loss – for failure, for missed experiences, for delays and boredoms – in this case the loss of the object as production, as art or otherwise, through the artist's hand or not.

Molesworth insists on the significance of the handmade quality of these 1964 editioned readymades that, aside from *Fountain*, were produced by craftspeople to mimic mass-produced objects – with *Fountain* mass-production is used to mimic mass-production. There is a cynicism (a boredom) in this gesture that she claims comes from the question of failure:

> If the Readymades of the 1910s and 1920s fail, insomuch as they can never quite be assimilated into the field of art proper, then the Readymades of the 1960s are 'good enough' Readymades, objects that accept the failure of the first go-round and deploy instead the strategy of the handmade as a way to ensure that the objects – part object, part sculpture – continue to have a kind of actuality, that they don't become 'symbolic' of something else, that they continue not to be mourned, but rather to be comfortably (visually) neglected, thrown into the healthy limbo that is 'the external world as perceived by two persons in common.'[6]

If the 'original' readymades fail at being art (I am not sure I agree with this), the remade readymades are able to achieve this object-oriented status not by simply accepting this failure but rather, I argue, through their compounding of it – turning failures into accelerations. That is, the editioned readymades transform objects into art objects through the enactment of the double failure at the core of modern aesthetics.

Far from betraying himself or the readymade as practice (production), the 1964 remades should be recognized as extending the core logic on which the readymades are founded: as always-already-replaceable products of a reproducible model. The readymades of one generation are replaced with the readymades of another generation, similar to the way an iPad or smartphone is repeatedly replaced by newer versions of itself – reflecting capitalist demands for the perpetual 'evolution' of consumer products (as quasi-values). Re-creating new versions of the readymades is therefore completely in line with this mode of art-making, one that, it must be remembered, is grounded not in the dichotomy of original and copy but rather functions through a logic of simulation. We might slightly extend Duchamp's claims about the readymade by observing not just its lack of uniqueness but also its lack of *difference*, the constructed objects from the Schwarz editions are capable of *delivering the same message* – enabling "the same 'metaphysical' value"[7] – as any other 'chosen' object of the model.

Such an understanding must also affect how we interpret the artworks produced in response to the readymade as practice. Instead of imitating the Duchampian readymade, artists such as Andy Warhol and Sherrie Levine are continuing the dynamic system of interpretations and re-interpretations that mark the successive advancement of the model. The question of the *can* (can a given object be art?) versus the *should* (should this object be art, in this time and in this place?) is paramount within the schema. Can Levine re-create *Fountain* as a bronze sculpture accompanied by its own museum plinth? – Yes, of course she *can*. However, for Duchamp the readymade aesthetic operates through the necessities of the *should* – should Levine's re-created *Fountain (after Marcel Duchamp)* be art, in the American culture of the 1990s, in our current cultural context under late (neoliberal) capitalism? In too many cases the only question asked is the *can*, which is a post-modern joke because the answer is always the same. Can Rachel Lachowicz re-make *Fountain* using women's cosmetic products or Huang Yong Ping re-make *Bottle Rack* as a large manifestation of a Buddhist Guan-Yin figure: yes. But there is no value in this yes. It can be repeated as an unlimited compulsion, which Duchamp recognized as a danger of "this form of expression" – 'art' in his opinion being "a habit forming drug" that his readymades must be protected against.[8] The question of the *should* locates value in the creative expenditure of judgment, the individual (as spectator) interpreting and re-interpreting the work to judge if it should be brought into contact with the external world, if it is (in that time and place) 'art'.

Too often the 'original' readymades are perceived and interpreted as single acts of creation, even when they consist of a number of such acts. *Fountain* is created in 1917, but it is also (re-)created in 1950, 1963 and 1964 – and we can extend this outward to include artists who complete the creative act started by Duchamp with their own creative acts, including Levine's 1991 *Fountain (After Marcel Duchamp)*, Lachowicz's 1992 *Untitled (Lipstick Urinals)* and, pushed somewhat to an extreme, Pope L.'s 2017 *Pedestal*. The relationship between artist and spectator is not a singular event. Rather it is, in potential, continually repeatable and transferable from one enactment to another, from one manifestation of a model to another, defining a dynamic system of interpreting and re-interpreting objects and art objects. The editioned readymades demonstrate the complex nature of the readymade aesthetic as already a re-perception and re-interpretation. An aesthetic that is not restricted to questions of just the readymades themselves, but extends into all forms of art objects and, more generally, all object-oriented relations. This is the vital terrain that is an accelerated Duchamp.

Notes

1 Marcel Duchamp to Robert Lebel, quoted in Kamien-Kazhdan, *Remaking the Readymade*, 159.
2 Schwarz, *The Complete Works of Marcel*, 834–839.
3 Kamien-Kazhdan, *Remaking the Readymade*, 149.
4 Duchamp to Philippe Collin, "Marcel Duchamp Talking about Readymades," 37–40.
5 Helen Molesworth, *Marcel Duchamp: By Hand, Even* (Cully: Kunsthalle Marcel Duchamp, 2017), 45–46.
6 Molesworth, *Marcel Duchamp: By Hand, Even*, 62.
7 Duchamp writes to the American artist Douglas Gorsline: "But signature or no signature your find has the same 'metaphysical' value as any other readymade, even has the advantage to have no commercial value." Duchamp, *Affectionately, Marcel*, 385.
8 Duchamp, "Apropos of 'Readymades'," 142.

16 We Will Wait

In his monumental re-creation of Duchamp's final installation, *Étant donnés* or *Given* (1946–1966), conceptual artist Serkan Özkaya presents a powerful enactment of Duchampian accelerationism. Not simply reproducing the work or attempting to make a *true copy* of it, there is a concerted effort in his project to speed up the material and ideational existence of the historical assemblage. He treats *Étant donnés* as an already existing (art)object – itself made of numerous ready-made forms and objects – that he translates in and through his own creative act, producing a version of the assemblage based within the model established by Duchamp.

Two significant points about *Étant donnés* should be remembered. First, Duchamp made the work over an approximately 20-year span, much of it in a secret studio, only sharing knowledge of the work with very select people. (Schwarz for example did not make the cut, which is why this major project is not included in the first edition of *The Complete Works of Marcel Duchamp*.) Second, the actual art object was put on display posthumously, being disassembled and reassembled with the help of a *Manual of Instruction* left by the artist for this exact purpose. A practical document, this manual demonstrates the parameters of the work (as model) by breaking it down into a series of objects and operations. When followed, these instructions communicated "the exact placement of every element to future custodians of his environmental assemblage," which was necessary since he knew "that the slightest margin of error would destroy the illusion he had so carefully devised."[1]

Using these instructions – along with a series of drawings by the architect Sandra Chollet[2] – Özkaya set himself to the task of remaking *Étant donnés*, not as a stand-in for the 'original' but rather as a speculative act of making this (art)object present; presented in the studio where Duchamp completed work on his final installation (see Figure 12). He approaches the assemblage as a constellation of readymades, objects and ideas that should be repeated and repeatable. Duchamp's *Manual of Instruction* supports such a belief, which requires an understanding of not just the art object (as whole) but also the individual elements (separate objects) that are the assemblage.

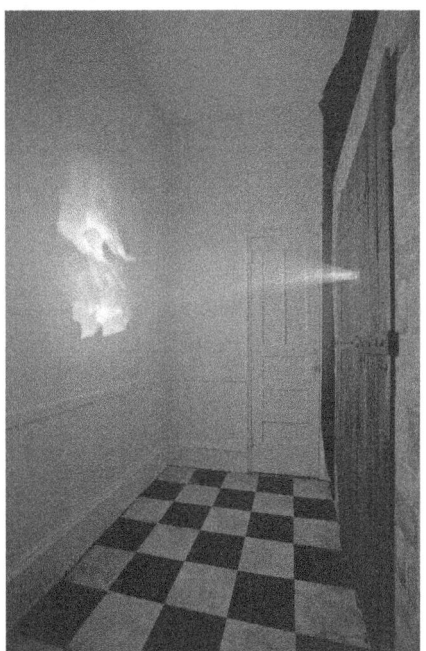

Figure 12 Serkan Özkaya, *We Will Wait*, 2014–2017 [exterior]. Mixed media assemblage. 416.5 x 345.4 x 633.7 cm. Installation view in Suit 403, 80 East 11th Street, New York City, USA.

Photo by Brett Beyer and Lal Bahcecioglu, courtesy of the artist.

For Duchamp, the *carefully devised illusion* of the work includes the *infrathin* failures that are part of the experience of viewing a nude woman holding up a gas lamp, partially exposed within a faux-landscape hidden behind a brick wall and a wooden door in a small darkened room that is part of the main Duchamp gallery, at the end of one wing of the Philadelphia Museum of Art. This elaborate illusion was clearly not meant to be convincing: I am not supposed to be fooled into believing this is an actual woman or an actual space. But the aesthetic failure – double failure with our active presence – is enlightening and supported by the intentional secrecy surrounding the work's production and final posthumous exhibition. For Özkaya this is not the end of *Étant donnés* but rather the fulfillment of its model, a readymade idea(l) that invites repeatability. This model reflects not a completed art object, not the final installation in Philadelphia, but rather a history of the work's existence as an idea and an object, a cosmology Özkaya recreates as the carefully devised simulation *We Will Wait* (2017).

Looking through the two peepholes in the wooden door – not Duchamp's aged door that he brought from Spain, but Özkaya's strangely faux-aged door that reminds me of its newness – I witness a scene that is uncanny in its overall likeness to the interior of *Étant donnés*. We see the exposed nude in her landscape still (or again) holding a gas lamp, the same model of Bec Auer lamp as the one used by Duchamp. Two apertures (optically) control our vision of her: the first are the eyeholes in the door through which we peep, and the second is the uneven opening in a wall that stands between the door and the figure. The internal lighting is carefully controlled in the general manner outlined by Duchamp in his *Manual of Instruction*. Taking a low-quality photograph through one of the holes I felt somewhat ridiculous, since the image captured so closely resembled images I had taken of the work in Philadelphia – raising the question, is Özkaya's *Étant donnés* capable of delivering the same message or enabling similar 'metaphysical' values as Duchamp's *Étant donnés*? While these likenesses are compelling, it is in the moments when Özkaya's version fails to conform with Duchamp's that we experience the model pushed beyond its initial aesthetic limits.

Looking through the peepholes in the oddly faux-aged door I encounter not a counterfeit of the 'original' or a reproduction that is part of a pure series, but rather a hyperreal – *infrathin* – experience that is also a missed (material and historical) experience (see Figure 13). The simulation is real: I touch the wooden door, feel the graininess of the clearly new(ish) wood, look past the (Styrofoam) faux-brick wall into the interior of the installation to see the decidedly unreal 3-D printed nude body. Özkaya could have easily used a door that gave the aura of age, or produced a nude that provided a cursory indication of the realism of the hidden nude in Philadelphia. But he did not.

Duchampian history is literally remade with new materials and modes of operation. Özkaya respects the basic parameters of the model Duchamp established while actively challenging and extending the possible futures of this model. With the help of the artist Fernán Nápoles, Özkaya transforms (aesthetically transubstantiates) the handmade life-size nude female body into digital readymade, a 3-D model that is, in potential, continually repeatable and transferable from one enactment to another, from one manifestation of a model to another.[3] Here the readymade aesthetic tests the line separating the objects used to produce what we might call an *uncertified untrue copy* of *Étant donnés* from the (re)creation of an art object, that of Özkaya's *Étant donnés*. This elaborate simulation is clearly not meant to be convincingly originary; I am not supposed to be fooled into believing this is *Étant donnés* or even a mere copy of Duchamp's final work. Rather the project has a self-conscious demeanor that is at once critical and playful, a very Duchampian reminder that art is only art for those who play along and believe in it.

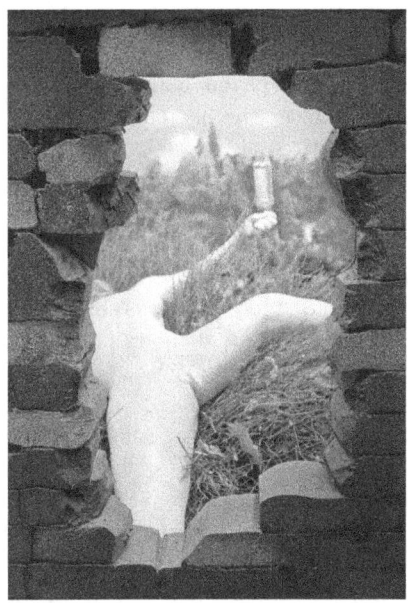

Figure 13 Serkan Özkaya, *We Will Wait*, 2014–2017 [interior]. Plastic sheeting, cardboard, Styrofoam, aluminum, clamps, wood, synthetic fiber wig, artificial white snow fluff, glue, blush, nail polish, acrylic paint, crayon, chalk, digital print, frosted Plexiglas, fluorescent lights, spot lights, 3D printed PLA, Auer-Welsbach burner, glass, twigs, leaves, paper, Philips Hue Bridge, Philips Hue App, Duvetyn, fabric, 3 RPM motor, LED lights, artificially weathered barn door, wallpaper, plastic panel, vinyl tiles, vellum, fishing line. 416.5 x 345.4 x 633.7 cm.

Photo by Serkan Özkaya, courtesy of the artist.

When Özkaya and I first met, he asked if I believed it was possible that Duchamp designed *Étant donnés* to secretly function as a type of camera obscura. This line of questioning has been explored before, specifically in response to the relationship between the dark room in which the viewer encounters the door and the extremely powerful light of the installation's interior. As with all elements of the assemblage, Duchamp meticulously planned the arrangement of each light used, providing a diagram on page 20 of the *Manual of Instruction* illustrating locations and even wattage of the light bulbs. Much like a traditional camera obscura, light passes through the aperture – in this case dual apertures – of the eyeholes into the darkened room; in Penelope Haralambidou's words, this is "a double camera obscura in reverse: not a dark chamber into which images of the outside world are projected, but a hidden, intensely lit and three-dimensional view that projects a pair of images outward."[4]

Özkaya positions the door of his assemblage at a particular distance from a wall in the actual space of exhibition, enabling a picture of this double projection to be made visible on its surface. (There are speculations that the projection forms a face, even a concealed self-portrait of Duchamp.) Testing the light from Duchamp's installation, Haralambidou holds up a sheet of paper at a length away from the eyeholes. She poetically describes this optical phantasm: "A rough trace of the outlines of the main shapes, pink for the flesh and blue for the sky, reveals the door's ability to draw an image of *Given* in light."[5] Özkaya takes this assessment further, exploring the possibility of a camera obscura by re-creating a scale version of the installation and enacting this alternate conceptual history.

More than this, he actively challenges the aesthetic limits of *Étant donnés* as object and art object. He explores the work by remaking (re-substantiating) its material existence in the time and space in which he lives, rethinking its existence in the 21st century – with a specific relationship to New York City, the same city where Duchamp constructed his final installation. With a happy irony, Özkaya initially installed the work in the actual space of Duchamp's 80 East 11th Street studio, inside the infamous suite number 403. This is the secret space where *Étant donnés* was completed, where Denise Brown Hare took her important series of photographs that show Duchamp's complex work as it appeared before it was moved to the Philadelphia Museum of Art. (When I stood in this exact space, now an apartment, I heard a dog in the residence above, experienced the lived environment of this site and almost expected Marcel himself to open the door and say, 'hope you have not been waiting long'.) Özkaya's project constructs a contradictory history that locates us outside of an (art)object that we are already truly inside. Experiencing *We Will Wait* one gets a strange sense of remembering a missed *rendezvous*, which imbues the whole project with a futurated nostalgia.

The readymade aesthetic is here shown to extend beyond questions of just the readymades themselves, instead functioning as a critical methodology for interpreting a range of objects and art object through the logic of simulation. Özkaya takes Duchamp's installation as a readymade idea (or ideal, or object, or series of objects) that he reimages as the experience of an event, which must always occur for us in the present. We might speak of this remade assemblage as a hyper-translation in which the entire cosmology of *Étant donnés* is problematized, made manifest as a profound moment of delay – transformed into a 'counderstanding' of choices and judgments. Özkaya goes to great lengths to create a work that reflects the construct of *Étant donnés*, but also accelerates its entire existence as art and as Duchamp's final work.

Notes

1 Michael R. Taylor, "D for Door," *Public* 56: Public Attendant A to Z, eds. Serkan Ozkaya and Robert Fitterman (2017): 34.

2 Introducing Chollet's illustrations, Özkaya writes: "In the end, her drawings, together with Duchamp's instructions, became an indispensable guide to the work." See Sandra Chollet, "I for Ikea," *Public* 56: Public Attendant A to Z: 80–83.

3 See Fernán Nápoles, "J for Just Maria," *Public* 56: Public Attendant A to Z: 84–85.

4 Penelope Haralambidou, *Marcel Duchamp and the Architecture of Desire* (Burlington: Ashgate, 2013), 95.

5 Haralambidou, *Marcel Duchamp and the Architecture of Desire*, 94–95.

17 An accelerated Duchamp

In his introduction to *Marcel Duchamp, Notes*, Paul Matisse observed: "Marcel used to say that explanations explained nothing. In fact, he thought so little of them that when others explained his work he usually agreed, even when they were wrong. He knew that even when we are right we only lose the world by explaining it, and that nothing, finally, is better than taking reality just as it comes."[1] Making his final installation *Étant donnés* public only after his death is perhaps Duchamp's greatest expression of this belief because such an act made sure there would never be an explanation (or more accurately there will always be a lack of explanation). Without any words by the artist, we, the spectators, are left completely to our own devices when deciphering and interpreting the work. Without any *given* meanings, we can only ever take the reality of the art object – or any object for that matter – as it comes to us, in our own time and place in the world.

Duchamp uses the discourse of art to challenge us to see that our reality is more than the object-oriented relationships given to us in consumer culture – ready-made choices that have built into them the (imposed) assumption of completeness. This is the choice economy that controls the possibilities of experience, providing a limited world of seemingly endless yet meaningless possibility and choice. Against this model, the readymade aesthetic demonstrates that the individual is capable of creating by choosing differently, by *creatively* (Nietzsche would say *wilfully*) choosing to push beyond socially and culturally prescribed experiences, meanings and values.

Duchampian accelerationism takes the realities of the object as conceived and experienced within consumer capitalism as a starting point for rethinking the practice of art in modern and contemporary culture, a critical project defined in and through the readymade as a mode of production. This is the readymade as an economy that accelerates modern aesthetics, and through it politics. That explores how notions of speeding up culture are materialized – made material – in subjective experiences of objects, embracing the aesthetic contradictions of objects and art objects within consumerist society. That confronts the impasse of globalized capitalist production by recognizing in the discourse of art a vital language with a capacity to challenge the foundation of our subjective relationship with (art)objects in our lives. This is the readymade not as *can* but as *should*: not the permissive *can it be art* but rather the necessities of asking *should it be art* (in this time and place).

If the readymade is an act of accelerating art as a discourse, we quickly discover that this speeding up also involves the realization of its opposite, an aesthetics of the ordinary (of boredom). Within the readymade mode of production the consequences of accelerationism are not increased speed and progress – a hallmark belief of Futurists and (so-called) 'post'-modernists alike – but rather an excessive experience of lack, personal and existential. For Duchamp the readymade as practice (as a philosophy of art) must accept, even celebrate, the acceleration of the object's ordinariness, which allows us to rethink the art object in relation to this gap. As Njabulo S. Ndebele eloquently states: "The ordinary is sobering rationality; it is the forcing of attention on necessary detail."[2] Duchampian accelerationism is the creative use of ordinary and everyday object-based relations as a means of production capable of maximizing the expenditure of individual critical judgment.

Through the readymade aesthetic, we can recognize an alternate economy of choices (as production), which empower us to creatively rethink their own sense of reality. This 'counderstanding' of opposites allows for the recognition of the individual's creative presence in the moment of an encounter with an object, a creative will within a world of consumer capitalist relations. Duchampian accelerationism is a model for aesthetically pushing beyond the perceived limits of aesthetic experience, for rethinking what it means to bring (art)objects into contact with our world.

The readymade aesthetic positions us to rethink the history of the art object and its relationship to objects in general. To rethink the art object's place in the world and to rethink an individual's relationship with objects and art objects, particularly in moments when this distinction fails. "Duchamp demonstrates that in order to act differently one must live differently and that in capitalism to do so doesn't depend on work but on its refusal, one which belongs to a different kind of ethics and a different 'anthropology'."[3] Duchampian accelerationism privileges the creative capacities of choice, which allow for an active refusal of all cultural, political and economic givens (pre-made choices) that relentlessly limit possible subjective meanings and values. And this includes the historical personage *Marcel Duchamp*, which is too often presented as if he were complete without us. I am proposing an accelerated Duchamp that, loosely defined, pushes to its most extreme the existing (given) understandings of his history, practice and conception of art, intensifying the possibilities he presents to us and believing we *should* individually complete and re-complete *Marcel Duchamp* by choosing and continually re-choosing who he is for ourselves.

Notes

1 Paul Matisse, Introduction, *Marcel Duchamp, Notes*, xv.
2 Njabulo S. Ndebele, "The Rediscovery of the Ordinary: Some New Writings in South Africa," Journal of Southern African Studies 12.2 (April 1986): 152.
3 Lazzarato, *Marcel Duchamp and the Refusal to Work*, 41.

Index

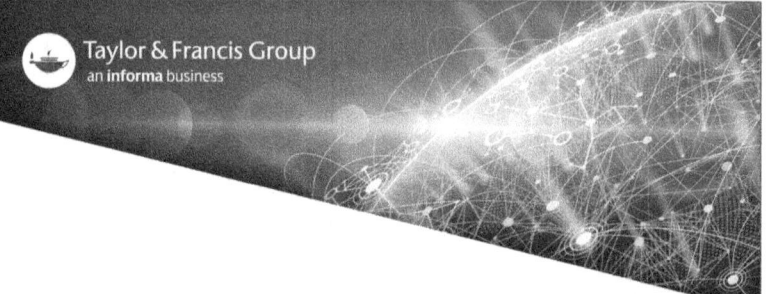
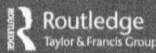
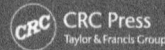

For Product Safety Concerns and Information please contact our EU
representative GPSR@taylorandfrancis.com
Taylor & Francis Verlag GmbH, Kaufingerstraße 24, 80331 München, Germany